State of
the World's
Minorities
2007

Acknowledgements

Minority Rights Group International (MRG) gratefully acknowledges the support of all organizations and individuals who gave financial and other assistance for this publication including the Sigrid Rausing Trust and the European Commission. Commissioning Editor: Richard Green

Minority Rights Group International

Minority Rights Group International (MRG) is a non-governmental organization (NGO) working to secure the rights of ethnic, religious and linguistic minorities and indigenous peoples worldwide, and to promote cooperation and understanding between communities. Our activities are focused on international advocacy, training, publishing and outreach. We are guided by the needs expressed by our worldwide partner network of organizations which represent minority and indigenous peoples.

MRG works with over 150 organizations in nearly 50 countries. Our governing Council, which meets twice a year, has members from 10 different countries. MRG has consultative status with the United Nations Economic and Social Council (ECOSOC), and observer status with the African Commission on Human and People's Rights. MRG is registered as a charity and a company limited by guarantee under English law. Registered charity no. 282305, limited company no. 1544957.

ISBN 1 904584 59 4
Published March 2007
Design by Texture +44 (0)20 7739 7123
Printed in the UK

Cover photo

A Tamil child living with her family in the damaged remains of Jaffna railway station, Sri Lanka, having been displaced by the civil war. Howard Davies/Exile Images

Inside cover photo

Dalit children collect wood in Uttar Pradesh, India. Ami Vitale/Panos Pictures

Minority Rights Group International
54 Commercial Street, London, E1 6LT, United Kingdom. Tel +44 (0)20 7422 4200, Fax +44 (0)20 7422 4201, Email minority.rights@mrgmail.org
Website www.minorityrights.org

Getting involved

MRG relies on the generous support of institutions and individuals to further our work. All donations received contribute directly to our projects with minorities and indigenous peoples.

One valuable way to support us is to subscribe to our report series. Subscribers receive regular MRG reports and our annual review. We also have over 100 titles which can be purchased from our publications catalogue. In addition, MRG publications are available to minority and indigenous peoples' organizations through our library scheme.

MRG's unique publications provide well-researched, accurate and impartial information on minority and indigenous peoples' rights worldwide. We offer critical analysis and new perspectives on international issues. Our specialist training materials include essential guides for NGOs and others on international human rights instruments, and on accessing international bodies. Many MRG publications have been translated into several languages.

If you would like to know more about MRG, how to support us and how to work with us, please visit our website www.minorityrights.org, or contact our London office.

Select MRG publications:
- *Assimilation, Exodus, Eradication: Iraq's minority communities since 2003*
- *Preventing Genocide and Mass Killing: The Challenge for the United Nations*
- *Minority Rights in Kosovo under International Rule*
- *Electoral Systems and the Protection and Participation of Minorities*

 This document has been produced with the financial assistance of the European Union. The contents of this document are the sole responsibility of Minority Rights Group International and can under no circumstances be regarded as reflecting the position of the European Union.

State of the World's Minorities 2007

Events of 2006

With a preface by Gay J McDougall,
UN Independent Expert on Minority Issues

Minority Rights Group International

Preface

Gay J McDougall,
UN Independent Expert on
Minority Issues

It is increasingly clear that ethnicity and religion are among the most potent mobilizing forces in societies. This is exacerbated in societies in which ethnicity and religion mark the fault lines between the haves and the have-nots, the powerful and the powerless, those who have hope and those who despair. In the past few months, this has been graphically illustrated by the turbulence in the Middle East – but, as this annual review by Minority Rights Group International shows, these tensions are commonplace around the world. However, it is important to emphasize that ethnic or religious diversity alone is neither a precondition for nor a determinant of violent conflict. The existence of minority groups in what may be perceived to be an otherwise homogeneous society is not an inherent cause of conflict.

While acknowledging the reality of ethnic or religious dimensions in many conflicts, the more fundamental causes of these conflicts generally lie below the surface, buried, often intentionally, by those with an interest in fomenting conflict. In some situations, the purveyors of war are actually seeking power and profits by immoral or illegal means, and they often find easy cover in deflecting blame onto those who are most powerless and most different. Also, in times of hardship, racism is often employed to divert attention from the root causes of despair. And targeting an easily identifiable group for exclusion or exploitation allows some to feel comfort in a mythology that dehumanizes certain people based on how they look or what they believe, the language they speak or where their ancestors called home.

Wars with ethno-religious components are deeply complex and must be better understood if we are to stand a chance of preventing, in this century, the bloodshed that marked the last. We must dispel the myth that diversity is, in itself, a cause of tension and conflict.

In contrast, we must promote the understanding that diverse societies can be among the healthiest, the most stable and prosperous. Respect for minority rights is crucial to this understanding. Minority rights are based on the principle of an integrated society, where each can use their own language, enjoy their culture and practise their religion while still embracing a broader, inclusive national identity.

The opportunity to participate fully and effectively in all aspects of society, while preserving group identity, is essential to true equality and may require positive steps on the part of governments. Minority rights are not about giving some communities more than others. Rather, they are about recognizing that, owing to their minority status and distinct identity, some groups are disadvantaged and are at times targeted, and that these communities need special protection and empowerment.

Equality for all does not always come naturally or easily when political power and influence over the institutions of state lie predominantly in the hands of certain groups, which, perhaps due to their majority status, have a political advantage. History has shown us, time and again, the immense damage caused to nations, peoples and regions by those who use the power at their disposal for the benefit of only some, while excluding or actively oppressing others as a means to maintain, entrench or extend their power.

For such societies, the exclusion, discrimination and resentment that are fostered by such power imbalance, create the conditions under which fault lines may occur along ethnic or religious grounds. It is perhaps here, in the fundamental flaws or dysfunctioning of governmental power, that the seeds of tensions and grievances are sown that later may emerge into conflicts. Such conflicts are misunderstood as being purely ethnic or religious conflicts, based upon difference and the perceived inability of different groups to live peacefully together. In fact they are often more correctly conflicts of greed and inequality than they are conflicts of diversity.

Today, in almost every corner of our world it seems that that there is a growing suspicion of 'otherness' or difference, whether it be ethnic, religious or based on other grounds. This climate of fear is also open to abuse by those who might seek to exploit divisions between different religious faiths, or those who might justify oppression in the name of security.

In this worrying climate, the principles enshrined in the UN Declaration on the Rights of National or Ethnic, Religious and Linguistic Minorities are as relevant today as ever, and as needed for healthy, diverse societies. In adopting this Declaration in 1992, states have pledged to protect the existence – and identity – of minorities within their territory, to establish conditions of equality and non-discrimination, and to ensure effective participation of minorities in public life. The Declaration is a benchmark – codifying the minimum treatment that those belonging to minority communities should expect from their governments. It is central to my mandate to promote implementation of this vital Declaration, and I pursue my work in the knowledge that, in doing so, I am also promoting conflict prevention; urging that injustices and inequities be identified at an early stage so that lasting solutions may be found.

Gay J McDougall

Peoples under Threat

Mark Lattimer

It is something of a paradox that, in the period from the aftermath of the Cold War to the early years of the 'war on terror', the world became, by most objective criteria, much safer. Certainly, the number of conflicts fought around the world has steadily fallen and, the great Congolese war apart, the total number of people who have died in them has decreased too. Each research institute compiles its figures somewhat differently, but most conflict experts recorded 20 or fewer major armed conflicts in 2006, compared to a high of over 30 in 1991. Of course, whether a community *feels* safe is as much a judgement about the future as an evaluation of the present. The recent use in Western states of emergency powers and other mechanisms curtailing civil liberties is a response to armed attacks in the USA, Spain and the UK which are in many respects unprecedented, although very rare. But the great toll of death from political violence continues in the countries of the South, in Africa, Asia and the Middle East, and today's wars have this in common with the ethno-nationalist conflicts that succeeded the fall of the Soviet Union: the violence is overwhelmingly targeted by ethnicity or religion. Wars as a whole may be less common, but in three-quarters of the major armed conflicts around the world in 2006, particular ethnic or religious groups were the principal target. In 2007, minorities have more cause than most to feel unsafe.

New threats in 2007

Minority Rights Group International (MRG) has used recent advances in political science to identify which of the world's peoples are currently under most threat. As explained in the last edition of *State of the World's Minorities*, academic researchers have identified the main antecedents to episodes of genocide or mass political killing over the last half century (see *State of the World's Minorities 2006*). Approximating those main antecedents by using current data from authoritative sources, including the World Bank, the Organization for Economic Cooperation and Development (OECD) and leading conflict prevention institutes, enables the construction of the Peoples Under Threat 2007 table (see p.11 for short version and Table 1, pp.118–22 in the Reference section for the full version). The indicators used comprise measures of prevailing armed conflict; a country's prior experience of genocide or mass killing; indicators of

group division; democracy and good governance indicators; and a measure of country credit risk as a proxy for openness to international trade.

The position of Somalia at the top of the table for 2006 attests to a highly dangerous combination of factors. In June 2006 the Union of Islamic Courts (UIC), an Islamic coalition seeking to restore law and order to Somalia, took over Mogadishu and subsequently much of the country, curbing the power of Somalia's warlords. However, in December, Ethiopian armed forces acting in support of the Transitional Federal Government (TFG), and supported by the USA, overthrew the UIC, which had received support from Eritrea and a number of Middle Eastern states. The TFG is unlikely to be able to retain control of the country without outside support. While one side has portrayed itself as fighting terrorists linked to al-Qaeda, and the other claims it is fighting Christian invaders, the most immediate fear is now a renewal of atrocities against civilians in the context of Darood–Hawiye inter-clan rivalry and a threat to minorities both in Somalia and in neighbouring Ethiopia. Although the UIC emphasized the importance of moving away from clan politics and had achieved some success in overcoming 'clanism', it was nonetheless particularly associated with the Hawiye clan. It also provided overt support for Oromo and Ogaden self-determination movements in Ethiopia. There is now a grave threat of violent repression against these populations, as well as other groups in Somalia in the context of a power vacuum and/or continued intervention by neighbouring states.

The situation in Iraq continues to deteriorate. Figures released by the United Nations (UN) based on body counts in Iraq's hospitals and morgues showed over 3,000 violent civilian deaths a month for most of the latter half of 2006. These were mainly comprised of killings by death squads, often linked to the Iraqi government itself; attacks by Sunni insurgent groups; and deaths in the context of military operations conducted by the Multinational Force in Iraq. The UN High Commissioner for Refugees estimates that between 40,000 and 50,000 Iraqis flee their homes every month. What is less well publicized is the particular plight of Iraq's smaller communities, the 10 per cent of the population who are not Shia Arab, Sunni Arab or Sunni Kurd. These minorities, which include Turkomans, Chaldo-Assyrians, Armenians,

Rank	Country	Group	Total
1	Somalia	Darood, Hawiye, Issaq and other clans; Bantu and other groups	21.95
2	Iraq	Shia, Sunnis, Kurds, Turkomans, Christians; smaller minorities	21.61
2	Sudan	Fur, Zaghawa, Massalit and others in Darfur; Dinka, Nuer and others in the South; Nuba, Beja	21.50
4	Afghanistan	Hazara, Pashtun, Tajiks, Uzbeks	21.03
5	Burma/ Myanmar	Kachin, Karenni, Karen, Mons, Rohingyas, Shan, Chin (Zomis), Wa	20.40
6	Dem. Rep. of the Congo	Hema and Lendu, Hunde, Hutu, Luba, Lunda, Tutsi/Banyamulenge, Twa/Mbuti	19.88
7	Nigeria	Ibo, Ijaw, Ogoni, Yoruba, Hausa (Muslims) and Christians in the North	19.22
8	Pakistan	Ahmadiyya, Baluchis, Hindus, Mohhajirs, Pashtun, Sindhis	18.97
9	Angola	Bakongo, Cabindans, Ovimbundu	16.68
10	Russian Federation	Chechens, Ingush, Lezgins, indigenous northern peoples, Roma	16.29
11	Burundi	Hutu, Tutsi, Twa	16.20
12	Uganda	Acholi, Karamojong	16.18
13	Ethiopia	Anuak, Afars, Oromo, Somalis	16.11
14	Sri Lanka	Tamils, Muslims	16.00
15	Haiti	Political/social targets	15.72
16	Côte d'Ivoire	Northern Mande (Dioula), Senoufo, Bete, newly settled groups	15.62
17	Rwanda	Hutu, Tutsi, Twa	15.31
18	Nepal	Political/social targets, Dalits	15.07
19	Philippines	Indigenous peoples, Moros (Muslims)	15.06
20	Iran	Arabs, Azeris, Baha'is, Baluchis, Kurds, Turkomans	15.02

Mandean-Sabeans, Faili Kurds, Shabaks, Yezidis and Baha'is, as well as a significant community of Palestinians, made up a large proportion of the refugees fleeing to neighbouring Jordan and Syria in 2006. In addition to the generalized insecurity they face, common to all people in Iraq, minorities suffer from specific attacks and threats due to their ethnic or religious status, and cannot benefit from the community-based protection often available to the larger groups.

With Somalia, Iraq and Afghanistan taking three out of the top four places in the table, and Pakistan rising eight places to be ranked eighth, the correlation between peoples under threat and the front lines in the US-led 'war on terror' is even starker than it was in 2005–6. The debate about whether US foreign policy on terrorism is making Americans safer or not continues to rage in the US, but it is now surely beyond doubt that it has made life a lot less safe for peoples in the countries where the 'war on terror' is principally being fought.

The most significant risers in the table in addition to Pakistan are listed below. Perhaps the most startling case is that of Sri Lanka, where peace talks failed and the conflict between the government and the Liberation Tigers of Tamil Eelam re-erupted, causing over a thousand civilian deaths and the displacement of hundreds of thousands in 2006 (see the report by Farah Mihlar). Civilians in Tamil areas are at particular risk, as is the country's Muslim population, which is caught between the two sides but was excluded from the peace negotiations.

Another long-running self-determination conflict that experienced a resurgence in 2006 was in Turkey, where a Kurdish splinter group carried out bomb attacks in major cities. It remains to be seen whether the ongoing negotiations over Turkey's accession to the European Union will temper the ambitions of some parts of the Turkish government and military to increase repression of the Kurds. In fact, Kurds throughout the region face heightened threats in 2007, with both Turkey and Iran massing troops on their respective borders with Iraq, claiming that Iraqi Kurdistan is being used as a base by armed Kurdish groups from which to launch attacks on their territory.

Iran's position in the top 20 does not relate solely to the threat against Iranian Kurds but also to the country's other minorities (including Ahwazi Arabs, Baluchis and Azeris), who in total constitute nearly 40 per cent of the population. Successive Iranian governments have been hostile to demands for greater cultural freedom for ethnic minority communities, and the US-led intervention in Iraq and the international stand-off over Iran's nuclear programme have left the government deeply wary of any perceived foreign involvement with minority groups. President Ahmadinejad has blamed British forces for being involved in 'terrorist' activities in Khuzistan, a mainly Arab province bordering southern Iraq.

The military coup in Thailand in September 2006 was effected without significant bloodshed, although Thailand's status as a popular Western tourist destination ensured it received widespread media coverage. Less well known is the fact that the coup followed an escalation in the conflict in the south of the country between the government and separatist groups, placing the mainly Muslim population in the southern border provinces at increased risk.

That both Lebanon and Israel and the Occupied Territories/Palestinian Authority have risen in this year's table comes as no surprise following the war between Israel and Hezbollah in 2006 and an escalation of Israeli military operations in the Occupied Territories. (Israel did not appear in last year's table due to the absence of data on some of the indicators.) Israel's bombardment of Lebanon fell particularly heavily on the Shi'a population, but the war has destabilized the country as a whole, placing all communities at the greatest risk since the early 1990s of a return to civil war. In Gaza, an Israeli offensive followed the kidnapping of an Israeli soldier in June, with a total of over 600 Palestinians killed in 2006 as a whole. Throughout the Occupied Territories/Palestinian Authority, the population faces an increased threat, not just from Israeli military operations but also from civil conflict between rival Palestinian factions.

Three states have fallen out of the top 20 in 2006: Indonesia, where a peace agreement signed in 2005 in Aceh has so far held, and Liberia and Algeria, both of which continue to recover following the civil wars that tore those countries apart in the 1990s.

Finally, it should be noted that although the number of African states in the top 20 has fallen slightly since 2005–6, Africa continues to account for half of the countries at the top of the table, making it still the world's most dangerous region for minorities.

Major risers since 2006

Rank	Rise in rank since 2006	Country	Group	Total
8	8	Pakistan	Ahmadiyya, Baluchis, Hindus, Mohhajirs, Pashtun, Sindhis	18.97
14	47	Sri Lanka	Tamils, Muslims	16.00
15	13	Haiti	Political/social targets	15.72
20	5	Iran	Arabs, Azeris, Baha'is, Baluchis, Kurds, Turkomans	15.02
33	12	Yemen	Political/social targets	12.63
35	7	Lebanon	Druze, Maronite Christians, Palestinians, Shia, Sunnis	12.25
39	15	Turkey	Kurds, Roma	12.02
40	7	Guinea	Fulani, Malinke	11.83
53	New entry	Thailand	Chinese, Malay-Muslims, Northern Hill Tribes	10.96
54	New entry	Israel/OT/PA	Palestinians in Gaza/West Bank, Israeli Palestinians	10.83

Participation as prevention

The identification of communities at grave risk around the world prompts the immediate question: what can be done to improve their situation? International action is considered later in this chapter; here, we concentrate on one factor at the national level which, perhaps more than any other, has the potential to address minority grievances and to prevent the development of violent conflict. The public participation of minorities, their active engagement in the political and social life of a state, underpins all other efforts to protect the rights of minorities and acts as a safety valve when major sites of disagreement between communities threaten to turn violent.

Within the state, public participation can take many forms, including, most importantly, representation in parliament (this is considered in more detail in Andrew Reynolds' chapter below) and in the executive branch of government, and participation in the judiciary, civil service, armed forces and police. More generally, it extends to taking part in the economic and social life of a state,

such that minorities feel they have a real stake in the society in which they live, that it is *their* society as much as that of anyone else. In areas where minority communities are geographically concentrated, it may also include a measure of autonomy or self-government.

In an important speech he made on a visit to Indonesia, the former UN Secretary-General Kofi Annan also made this point when he was commenting on the extreme case of separatism.

'Minorities have to be convinced that the state really belongs to them, as well as to the majority, and that both will be the losers if it breaks up. Conflict is almost certain to result if the state's response to separatism causes widespread suffering in the region or among the ethnic group concerned. The effect then is to make more people feel that the state is not their state, and so provide separatism with new recruits.'

Even within one state, very different responses to claims for regional autonomy can develop. In India, for example, the positive approach shown to managing decentralized governance in Tamil Nadu can be contrasted with the state's hostility towards autonomy claims in Punjab, Kashmir and Nagaland. In the Russian Federation, the accommodation of autonomy in a region such as Tatarstan can similarly be contrasted with the gross human rights violations that continue to be committed in Chechnya in the name of combating separatism. Each situation is of course different, but it is notable that, in the case of Indonesia itself, perhaps the most significant faller in this year's Peoples under Threat table, the national parliament in July 2006 adopted a framework for autonomy that will enable the first direct local elections to be held in the region of Aceh, the scene of nearly three decades of separatist conflict. Since a pact was signed in August 2005, the Free Aceh Movement has reportedly dissolved its armed wing and the Indonesian government has withdrawn troops from Aceh.

But, in many states, it is public participation at the national level that constitutes the key issue for minority protection and conflict prevention. Here it is worth making a distinction between the formal mechanisms of participation, such as elections, and having a genuine say in how a country is run (the former being a necessary but not sufficient condition for the latter). That Iraq has been pushed from the top of the list in this year's table is due to a

slightly less negative showing under the cited World Bank governance indicators, particularly for 'Voice and Accountability', a measure of the extent to which citizens of a country are able to participate in the selection of governments, including an assessment of the political process and human rights (note that the indicators were published in September with a nine-month lag). Yet the fact that Iraqi citizens were able to participate in elections and that the main communities are all represented in government has not prevented the polity from being fatally fractured. The same could be said of Bosnia and Herzegovina, which remains stubbornly alongside Serbia in the upper part of the table, despite over a decade having passed since the power-sharing deal established under the Dayton Peace Agreement. It is clear that the international community still has a lot to learn about the application of public participation in practice.

For public participation to help reduce the threat of violent conflict it needs to be more than simply an entry ticket to a shouting match. It needs to constitute participation *in governance*, and that in turn depends on a basic level of governmental effectiveness and rule of law. However, in both Iraq and Bosnia the mechanisms for community representation introduced under international control have themselves exacerbated or entrenched the division of the state on ethnic or sectarian lines, and induced a level of state failure. Following the occupation of Iraq in 2003, the coalition authorities established an Iraqi Governing Council in which membership was strictly apportioned along ethnic and sectarian lines. Political patronage ensured that whole ministries became dominated by officials from the minister's own sect or group, and sectarian politics quickly became the defining feature of the new Iraqi state. This mistake was compounded at the first Iraqi elections in January 2005, when the electoral system based on a national list combined with a boycott in Sunni Arab governorates effectively ensured that Sunni Arabs were largely excluded from political representation during a key year in the country's attempted transition to democracy. In other states with a long history of ethnic conflict, such as South Africa or Nigeria, constitutional and electoral mechanisms have been established which aim to promote inclusive political systems, with representation across ethnic or religious communities.

The subject of political participation and community representation in very divided societies merits further study, given its fundamental importance to peace-building and stability, and the focus on participation in this edition of the *State of the World's Minorities* is intended as a contribution. But just a brief review of country situations illustrates the obvious danger of constitutional or electoral systems which make ethnicity or religion a principal mobilizing factor in politics, leading to the creation of a majority or dominant group which is defined by ethnicity or sect.

This should be contrasted with the growing range of examples, some quoted above, of where effective participation of minorities has helped to resolve or prevent conflict, through the promotion of more inclusive political systems, whether at national or regional level. In addition to power-sharing agreements, a wide range of mechanisms are available to promote such participation appropriate to the given situation, including rules or incentives for political parties to appeal across communities, the adoption of electoral systems that favour rather than marginalize minorities, systems of reserved seats, special representation, formal consultative bodies, formal or informal quotas in public administration, and positive action programmes, as well as arrangements for greater self-government in regions where minorities are geographically concentrated.

Given the very high correlation around the world between minority status and poverty, it should also become a priority for international development agencies to promote the participation of minorities in their programmes, particularly at national and local level. It is now widely accepted that anti-poverty initiatives are unlikely to achieve long-term success unless the poor are closely consulted and involved in their formulation and delivery, yet minorities are typically excluded from the planning of development programmes, often through the same societal discrimination that is the root cause of their impoverishment in the first place. This is one reason why development programmes, while often bringing important benefits to a society, rarely succeed in targeting effectively the poorest communities.

The international response
After the hopes raised by the UN World Summit in September 2005, the international response in 2006

to the situation of peoples under threat can only be described as disappointing.

The headline case during 2006 continued to be the mass, ongoing crimes under international law committed against the population of the Darfur region of Sudan, which the Sudanese government is manifestly failing to protect. The World Summit resolved that, in such cases, the UN Security Council should be 'prepared to take collective action' in a manner that is 'timely and decisive'. In the event, the reaction of the Security Council was seen to be belated and divided. The strategy of the Sudanese government has been to emphasize its cooperation with the existing African Union (AU) mission in Darfur – while on the ground effectively controlling the AU forces' access to much of the region – and to oppose the deployment of any stronger UN force, relying on divisions in the Security Council and in particular the support of China, a major trading partner and heavy investor in the Sudanese oil industry. In August 2006, the Security Council did finally approve a 20,000-strong UN force, but Sudan continues to withhold consent for its deployment. Meanwhile, the situation in Darfur has deteriorated and continuing attacks by Sudanese armed forces and Janjaweed militia on civilian targets threaten to push the death toll far beyond the 200,000 that have already perished.

A measure of what international peacekeeping forces can achieve was demonstrated during 2006 in neighbouring Democratic Republic of Congo, where the UN's largest peacekeeping force oversaw the successful conclusion of the country's first free elections for 45 years, a major milestone on the road to peace. However, despite a new readiness on the part of the UN peacekeepers to react robustly to threats from militia groups, armed conflict continued in the east in both Ituri and Kivu (leaving the position of the Congo unchanged, near the top of the Peoples under Threat table).

In the programme of UN reform initiated at the World Summit in 2005, the most important development for human rights was the replacement of the discredited Commission on Human Rights with a new Human Rights Council. The vision was for a smaller body that would meet more often, combining improved expertise and objectivity with greater clout within the UN system. By the end of 2006, however, uncertainty still prevailed over the *modus operandi* of the Council's two main tools: the

new system of Universal Periodic Review, by which states' human rights records would be assessed by their peers, and the Council's special rapporteurs and working groups, with the future of the country rapporteurs called into question. More worryingly still, the Council quickly attracted accusations of political bias, and even criticism from the UN Secretary-General, after it held two special sessions devoted to the situation in Gaza and one to the Israel–Hezbollah conflict, but failed to look critically at other major cases of human rights violations around the world. It finally held a special session on Darfur in December, but passed a weak resolution, authorizing a high-level mission to assess the human rights situation but failing to recognize the culpability of the Sudanese government for the abuses committed in Darfur. This was despite the fact that indisputable links between the government and the militias responsible for much of the killing had been reported almost two years earlier by the International Commission of Inquiry on Darfur established by the UN Security Council.

Two recently established UN mechanisms have, however, played an important role in protecting minorities. The Independent Expert on Minority Issues has consistently highlighted minority protection issues worldwide, including issuing communications on the situation of Haitians in the Dominican Republic and on minority women in Burma (Myanmar). The Special Adviser to the UN Secretary-General on the Prevention of Genocide has undertaken two missions to Darfur, one to Côte d'Ivoire and one to the Thai–Burmese border to investigate events in Burma's Karen state following an intensification of Burmese military operations from November 2005 onwards. The Special Adviser makes recommendations concerning civilian protection, establishing accountability for violations, the provision of humanitarian relief and steps to settle the underlying causes of conflict.

The outgoing Secretary-General, Kofi Annan, established in May an Advisory Committee on the Prevention of Genocide to provide guidance to the Special Adviser and to contribute to the UN's broader efforts to prevent genocide. The committee's report, which has not been published, is believed to recommend strengthening the role of the Special Adviser by ensuring he report directly to the Secretary-General, improve his access to the Security Council and increase resources to the office, as well as calling for improved cooperation within and outside the UN system to obtain information specifically focused on early warning of genocide and other crimes against humanity. The recommendations have been sent to the incoming Secretary-General, Ban Ki-moon, and his response will be an early test of the new Secretary-General's commitment to improving civilian protection from mass atrocities.

The principal normative development during 2006 was the finalization of the Declaration on the Rights of Indigenous Peoples, which had occupied the UN Commission on Human Rights for over a decade. At its first meeting in June, the Human Rights Council approved a text of the Declaration that recognized indigenous peoples' rights to live in freedom, peace and security; not to be subjected to forced assimilation, destruction of their culture or forced population transfer; and recognized their rights to self-determination and self-government in matters relating to their internal and local affairs, and to practise their languages and cultural traditions.

However, in November the third committee of the UN General Assembly passed a procedural motion blocking approval of the Declaration, at least until later in 2007. The motion was put forward by Namibia on behalf of the African group on the committee and promoted by states including Canada, the USA, Australia and New Zealand, which had claimed during the debate that the Declaration may negatively affect the interests of other sectors of society. Although the Declaration's force would essentially have been hortatory and not legally binding, the motion was interpreted as an attempt to weaken the document or to ditch it altogether.

The failure to approve the Declaration is illustrative of a widespread refusal by states to recognize the special, and often very dangerous, position in which indigenous peoples and minorities more generally find themselves, and their urgent need for better international protection. Even affluent states that are free of internal armed conflict and whose territorial integrity remains unchallenged – whatever other security threats they face – frequently ignore the extent of discrimination faced by minorities and often indulge in a tendency to blame any community dispute or integration problem on the minority community itself. As the UN Special Adviser on the Prevention of Genocide

wrote in the *State of the World's Minorities 2006*, 'Governments in both the South and the North persist in labelling some people a threat simply because they are members of a minority.' Yet any assessment of prevailing conflicts and human rights violations around the world indicates that it is minorities themselves who are at greatest risk, usually at the hands of their own governments. Without the political courage to admit that reality, and to respond appropriately, the world is unlikely to become a safer place for minorities any time soon. ∎

Sri Lanka Flash Point

Farah Mihlar

The coastal route to Galle is a picturesque one. In the 115 km trip south from the Sri Lankan capital, Colombo, the view of the sparkling, blue Indian Ocean is almost uninterrupted. Fishermen return with their day's catch; bustling, roadside markets line the verges; girls in crisp white uniforms, with black, plaited hair scurry off to school. Unsurprisingly, the resorts in and around the southern port town are some of the country's top tourist destinations, drawing visitors from around the world.

The scenes are relaxed, even idyllic. But on Boxing Day 2004, Galle was one of the towns that was ravaged by the tsunami that ripped through most of Sri Lanka's coastline, reducing entire villages to rubble and killing some 40,000 people. Sri Lankans like me, who saw the waves crash in, and lived through those terrible days, have them etched in our memories. The panic, the horror, the grief of the bereaved were also played and replayed on television stations across the world. Though less in the international limelight, many families remained displaced in camps as we set out to drive to Galle to report on the plight of the tsunami victims, two years after the disaster.

But, on approaching the town, Sri Lanka's recurring nightmare of the past 20 years was about to engulf us. Not a natural disaster, but a man-made one. A catastrophe that has ripped apart this pear-shaped island in the Indian Ocean and blighted the lives of successive generations of Sri Lankans.

The first sign is the panic. A mass frenzy of people, mobbing vehicles, blocking our way forward. A bamboo pole is hoisted across the road as a flimsy barrier. Young men surround us, banging windows telling us to go back. The driver nervously lowers the shutters.

Left: A soldier stands guard near the site of the suicide bomb attack in Colombo, Sri Lanka, in December 2006.

'The Tigers are attacking Galle. There is firing all over. You'll be killed,' someone shouts through the window.

In the mêlée, we can barely comprehend the news. Everyone knew that Sri Lanka's stuttering peace process between the government and the Liberation Tigers of Tamil Eelam (LTTE) was about to collapse. But, even in the worst of times during the two-decade war, the southern coast was rarely attacked. Galle, like most southern towns, remained largely unscathed through all the big battles, which were confined to the country's north and east.

We draw into the side of the road, and wait nervously in the blazing sun. We turn on the radio. It tells of an audacious assault by the Tamil Tigers on the Galle port and adjoining naval base. Two rebel boats, carrying suicide bombers had launched an attack – prompting the navy to retaliate. Reports on the radio keep referring to the battle, just a few hundred metres away from where we are parked. Two people are reported killed.

We turn back and attempt another route. We make it to the nearby village of Katugoda, where dozens of children were orphaned, women widowed and livelihoods lost, when the tsunami struck. But now, to add to their misfortune, the war has arrived practically in their backyard.

'We heard four loud bangs, and went running out,' says Fauzun Nizam, a social worker who had been meeting with tsunami widows, when the Tigers' attack happened. 'Our hearts were pounding. I did not know what was happening. I thought "Oh God! Why?" First the tsunami and then this,' she adds.

The attack sent jitters across Sri Lanka. It brought home the painful reality that, after four years of relative peace, the war had returned. The ceasefire agreement signed between the government of Sri Lanka and Tamil Tigers in 2002 was in tatters. At the time, the deal was hailed by the international community and embraced by the war-weary people. For the first time in decades, Sri Lankans from the south were able to travel to the north and east. Food and clothes started to flow to the war-torn areas, banks and businesses opened new branches. Property began to boom, mainly propelled by expatriate Sri Lankans most of whom had fled the country as refugees.

But the euphoria didn't last long. Distrust between the government and Tamil Tigers, extremist stances by both parties and the rebels' lack of commitment to a negotiated settlement to the conflict, saw the peace process slowly crumble. The situation was further complicated by a historic split within the Tamil Tigers movement, which the Tigers' leadership felt was being exploited by the government.

Muslim minorities under attack

The impact of the resurgent conflict is being felt all over Sri Lanka. Almost half-way between Galle and Colombo lies the town of Aluthgama. School-teacher Mehroonniza Careem and her family fled here after heavy fighting erupted in the war-torn north-eastern town of Muttur in July 2006. The Muttur battle is considered by many to be the moment that sealed the end of the ceasefire. Mrs Careem is the principal of a well-known Muslim girls' school in the area. She is a dignified, strong-minded woman, but even she shudders as she recalls how the town came under attack by the Tigers and the government launched a fierce counter-offensive.

'First we heard huge blasts through the night, none of us could sleep, we were terrified, we could hear the explosions just near our house.'

Mrs Careem sought refuge in her school only to find that thousands of others had done the same.

'We were like matchsticks in a matchbox, each person stuck against the other, heads touching legs,' she says.

But the civilians sheltering in the school were not spared. Mrs Careem says the Sri Lankan army attacked the buildings, claiming that the rebels had infiltrated the complex. 'People fled, hoping to get to another town,' she says. 'We later heard some of them were killed by the Tigers.'

Mrs Careem did not just lose her home in the upsurge of violence – her beloved second son has gone too. Just days before the Muttur attack, he disappeared – allegedly kidnapped by the rebels – his whereabouts now unknown. When we meet, it is Ramadan, a holy month for Muslims. Mrs Careem is putting her faith in God, for the return of her 24-year-old son, Ramy. She cannot speak of her child, without breaking down. 'My son is mentally unwell. He has to take medication every day, otherwise he becomes very sick. I am pleading with them to release him.'

The toll exacted by Sri Lanka's decades' long civil war has been immense. It has cost more than

60,000 lives and displaced hundreds of thousands of civilians. There have been multiple human rights violations, rapes, and thousands of people have 'disappeared'. The causes of the conflict are complex – but the war pits the Tamil Tigers against the Sinhalese-dominated government of Sri Lanka.

The Sinhalese Buddhists, who make up 70 per cent of Sri Lanka's population, control the state machinery – the military as well as the government. The Tamils – the majority of whom are Hindus – are ethnically distinct and speak their own language. The rebel movement, the Tamil Tigers, want to carve out a separate state for minority Tamils in the north and east of the country.

Minority suffering ignored

But trapped in the middle, often ignored in the reporting of the Sri Lankan conflict, are the other minority communities. After Tamils, Muslims are the second largest minority in Sri Lanka – numbering nearly a million. They have suffered tremendously in the conflict but they are often the 'forgotten minority' and their plight is rarely acknowledged.

Sri Lankan Muslims are scattered across the country, but a majority live in the coastal areas. Their presence is a throwback mainly to the Arab-Indian traders who married local women and settled in the island many centuries after the Sinhalese and Tamils. Their dominance in eastern Sri Lanka – in some small towns they form the majority – and their insistence on their separate and unique identity has brought them into conflict with the Tamil Tigers, who see the Muslim presence as a hindrance to their homeland claim.

One of the most horrific episodes occurred in October 1990, when the Tigers engaged in a campaign to 'ethnically cleanse' areas they controlled. Nearly 100,000 Muslims were given 24 hours to leave. Most fled, taking nothing with them, forced into flimsy boats in the monsoon deluge. Crowded and panicked, some families lost their infant babies, who fell into the sea. The purge ripped apart Tamil and Muslim communities, who had previously lived peacefully side by side.

'I remember how we left, our Tamil neighbours crying, helpless, seeing us leave,' says Juwairiya Uvais, who was a young girl at the time. 'Hundreds and hundreds of people were all walking from different villages towards the beach.'

Juwairiya, her family and many others escaped to

the north-western town of Puttalam – the closest point that offered relative safety.

Yet, 16 years on, families still live in what were intended to be temporary camps. Juwairiya – who now works for a local charity – showed me around some of them. It was a stormy day, and we struggled to enter homes through flooding muddy pathways. Half built with bricks, topped with thatched roofs, the families call these dwellings their homes. But not a single individual I spoke to could produce a legal document to claim ownership of the land.

In the backyards, little children in tattered clothes chased chickens, while water dripped through the dry coconut-palm leaf roofs. Poverty is entrenched. Many Muslims driven from their homes in 1990 were left penniless. Well-to-do businessmen were reduced to working as labourers at onion farms. During Ramadan, Juwairiya helps to coordinate large sums of money traditionally given as charity in this month by wealthy Muslims in Colombo. 'There was a time we used to give charity, now for the last so many years we are recipients,' she says.

The renewed conflict has also added to the uncertainty surrounding people's lives. In Puttalam, as elsewhere in the country, more military checkpoints have sprung up as the authorities seek to crack down on the rebels' activities. When we are stopped at one of them, Juwairiya struggles to explain who she is to the Sinhala-speaking soldiers. There are a few tense moments. Juwairiya is not carrying the proper identity papers and, as she comes from the north-east, she speaks Tamil. In the current jittery climate, these two factors might be enough to get her arrested. Luckily, she is wearing a headscarf and, after a few moments discussion, the soldiers accept that she is Muslim, working with the displaced community, and wave her on.

It is not just Muslims who find themselves struggling to build new lives for themselves in Puttalam. Sinhalese Christians were also pushed out by the Tigers during the purge of the north-east. The Christians are Sri Lanka's smallest religious minority, found in both the ethnic Tamil and Sinhalese communities, and who mostly converted during the 400-year colonial occupation of the island by the Portuguese, Dutch and British.

Many of the displaced Christians in Puttalam live in one camp, close to the sea. The men eke out a living as fishermen, but, poor as they are, their futures are now even more precarious. The Galle attack was just one illustration of the rebels' capacity to launch sea-borne attacks. With the resumption of the war, the authorities have imposed harsh restrictions on sea travel. For fishermen, this means that they cannot set sail early in the morning.

'They tell us we can only go after 5:30 in the morning. There are no fish to catch at that time. We have to start much earlier,' says fisherman Herbert Jones.

Even if the rules were relaxed, Mr Jones believes that the fishermen living in the displaced people's camp, would still come off worse. 'The sea is supposed to belong to everyone but we don't belong to the village so we don't get to fish.'

Four hours' drive to the south, in the capital Colombo, at first glance, it seems as if it is a different world. Despite the renewed war, the city centre – as always – displays an amazing sense of resilience, ticking on despite the gloom. Hotels host parties most nights, restaurants are bursting with customers and the city bustles with an almost surreal sense of normalcy.

Behind the façade, however, you see a city under siege. Armed soldiers are everywhere, standing at temporary barricades with red Stop signs, flagging down vehicles to be checked for explosives. In 2006, Colombo has had more than five targeted bomb blasts, mainly aimed at opponents of the Tamil Tigers.

Traditionally, moderate Tamils have been singled out by the Tigers, who have a reputation for not tolerating political opposition from among their own ethnic community. In August 2005, Foreign Minister Lakshman Kadirgamar, an ethnic Tamil, was shot dead by a sniper at his home. In August 2006, Kethesh Loganathan, also a Tamil and deputy head of the government's peace secretariat, was shot dead. No one was ever brought to justice for those murders – but they were widely assumed to have been carried out by the Tamil Tigers.

Tamils targetted by military

During the conflict, Tamil moderates have found themselves doubly victimized. Vulnerable to rebel reprisals, they are also attacked by government forces, who believe them to be rebels or supportive of the Tamil Tigers. Under the terrorism laws, the ill-treatment of Tamils, subjected to illegal detention and torture, is well-documented. Moreover, Tamils in lower-class groups face routine harassment – something that has become more pronounced over the past few months.

The story of Janaki Sinnaswami, who is 59, is all too common. A Tamil who makes a living as a domestic worker in the wealthy houses of Colombo, she and her family have borne the brunt of Sri Lanka's bitter ethnic conflict. Her first home was destroyed in the infamous 1983 riots, when Sinhala mobs, with political backing, went on a rampage destroying Tamil houses, shops and businesses in all the main cities, and attacking Tamil families, killing, raping and injuring.

It was the first time an entire minority community was targeted and attacked in such a brutal and widespread manner, and is widely seen as the precursor to all-out war between the Tamil Tigers and the government. For Janaki, the loss of her home was a setback from which the family never recovered. Her family moved back to the crowded parental home in the slums, where seven adults and six children were cooped up in one room. Her husband – unable to cope – became an alcoholic and died. With no money to educate her oldest son, he grew up illiterate. Incredibly, against all the odds, Janaki scraped together the money from her work as a maid and succeeded in educating her two youngest children.

But now, with the collapse of the peace process, things have again taken a turn for the worse. In the slums, the military are again raiding the houses of Tamils.

'They bang on our doors at midnight hours. Army men come with guns and they check our entire house, open everything, ask us who we are

Below: A woman who fled from the town of Muttur prepares to make morning tea near a tent at the Al Aysha refugee camp in Kantale in August 2006.

harbouring,' Janaki says. 'I have told my mistress I can't work late, I have to go home because I have a young daughter and they can do anything to her when I am not at home.'

But if the situation for Tamils in Colombo is bad, in the war-torn north, it is much worse. In 2006, the renewed fighting claimed 3,000 lives – the majority of them in the north and east. Over the years, these areas have been shattered by the conflict. They are heavily mined in places, with little paths wending across a dry, barren landscape; families have been forced to flee their homes time

and time again. In the recent fighting, the situation has bordered on catastrophic, with the north effectively cut off from the rest of the country – the main roads have been blocked. At least one UN convoy carrying humanitarian supplies into the north-east had to turn back because of heavy fighting, with officials warning that the situation in some places was 'desperate'.

'In some areas people are moving to starvation, but what is food compared to human dignity?' says Revd Dr Rayappu Joseph, the Bishop of Mannar, in the north-west. The bishop is a well-known – but controversial – human rights activist. He is often attacked in the nationalist press for his alleged links to the Tamil Tigers, an accusation he staunchly denies. Shuttling between government and Tamil-

controlled areas the bishop has first-hand information on the plight of the people. He tells stories of young men being shot down or kidnapped under suspicion of being involved with the Tigers. He claims the killings often occur close to military or police checkpoints. Other human rights activists in the area, who refused to be identified, fearing for their lives, corroborate the information.

In December 2006, the government gave the security forces sweeping powers to search, arrest and question suspects. The fear is that these draconian measures could result in even more people being arrested and held incommunicado. As the crisis deepens, Bishop Joseph says, 'We are helpless people. There is no one to help us, there is no one to save us.'

With the resurgence in the conflict, the ghosts of the past have returned to haunt Sri Lanka. White vans, the horrifying symbol attached to disappearances in the early 1980s, have come back. The vans appear at the doorstep of homes in broad daylight, hauling in men and young boys as petrified families look on.

The University Teachers for Human Rights (UTHR), one of Sri Lanka's best-known human rights groups, accused the Tamil Tigers in a report published in June 2006. 'Fathers are huddled in their homes with their children fearing to go out, lest they are dragged into a van by thugs and are not seen again,' the report says.

In previous reports, the UTHR pointed the finger at the government, reporting on incidents where the military, in collusion with renegade Tamil groups, have been involved in abductions and killings.

Statistics are hard to come by, but in the month of September alone, just in the northern town of Jaffna, Sri Lanka's Human Rights Commission received 41 complaints of abductions. The men who are kidnapped rarely return; what happens to them remains a mystery. Although often presumed dead, years may pass without any official or rebel acknowledgement of the killing. Bodies may never be returned to grieving families.

The boys who are abducted are forced to take up arms. Since May 2006 UNICEF has received 135 reports of children being abducted to fight for Tamil militants in the war. And there are accusations that the government is implicated in child kidnappings too. Although it denies involvement with the dissident Tamil armed groups, the credibility of those denials was dealt a blow in November 2006,

when the government's position was contradicted by a senior UN official.

Following a visit to Sri Lanka, Allan Rock, a special adviser to the UN representative for children and armed conflict, said he 'found strong and credible evidence that certain elements of the Government security forces are supporting and sometimes participating in the abductions and forced recruitment of children'. His findings were an embarrassment to the government, which had always claimed to hold the moral high ground over the Tamil Tigers by accusing them of using child soldiers. It was this fact, combined with other human rights violations, that resulted in a ban on the Tamil Tigers and their political and fundraising activities in most Western states.

For many Sri Lankans, the collapse of the peace process and resurgence of violence has marked a terrifying new chapter in Sri Lanka's conflict-ridden history. One of the biggest fears is that it is now impossible to say who is responsible for the killings and abductions. Is it the government, is it paramilitary groups, is it the Tamil Tigers, or is it renegade factions? In 2006, several Tamil journalists, academics and peace activists with different affiliations have randomly been gunned down in a sinister string of killings that point to numerous perpetrators. Even more worrying, no one has been tried or found guilty for these crimes.

'Today the alarm is sounding for Sri Lanka. It is on the brink of a crisis of major proportions,' said Phillip Alston, the UN Special Rapporteur on extra-judicial killings, to the UN General Assembly in October 2006. But many Sri Lankans feel that such appeals are falling on deaf ears – that the world is not interested in their plight. With no vast oil reserves, or strategic importance to world powers, Sri Lankans feel they are being left to face a bleak future by themselves. As Lalith Chandana, a Christian fisherman living in the Puttalam camp, puts it, 'Every day we hear about peace but … we have no hope peace will come.'

Colombo, November 2006

Public Participation by Minorities
Minority Members of the National Legislatures

Andrew Reynolds

When the first democratic National Assembly convened in Cape Town, South Africa, in 1994 it was the living embodiment of Archbishop Desmond Tutu's dream of a 'rainbow nation': an Assembly that was not merely elected by all but included all. Black sat with white on the government's benches, coloured MPs joined with Afrikaners in opposition. But, beyond that, the Assembly of 1994 contained Ndebele, Pedi, Tswana, Sotho, Venda, Xhosa and Zulu, along with Indian South Africans, Anglo-whites, Afrikaans-speaking Cape coloureds and Afrikaans speakers of Dutch or French Huguenot descent. The descendants of Mohandas Gandhi, Henrik Verwoerd and Govan Mbeki sat together, side by side.

South Africa's ethos of political inclusion has waned a little over the past 12 years, but the over-representation of minority groups still remains the norm. While the inclusion of minorities is less visible in most other parts of the world, there is not a nation-state, rich or poor, democratic or not, where minority groups do not press for their voices to be heard at the highest levels of decision-making. Most countries seek to create at least a small space for minorities in their national parliaments: there are Christians and Samaritans in the Palestinian Authority, Maoris in the New Zealand house, nomadic Kuchi in the Afghan Wolesi Jirga, German-speaking MPs in Poland, and Roma members of the Romania parliament. Whether these representatives are enough, have influence on government policy, or are even *representative* of the minority groups they come from, are crucial questions, but when minority communities have no representatives in national legislatures we can be pretty sure that those minority groups are not being heard in the policy dialogue, their rights are being disregarded and their importance in electoral competition is small.

In many respects, the question of promoting minority representation is akin to the attention increasingly being paid to ensuring the participation of women in politics. There are now more women MPs around the world than ever before and an ever growing number of countries that use special mechanisms to increase their number of women MPs. While the question of how best to promote minority representation has received far less attention, it is an evolving issue for both international organizations and nation-states seeking

to build more stable and inclusive societies. In fragile and divided societies, ensuring that a significant number of minority MPs are elected is a necessary, if not sufficient, condition of short-term conflict prevention and longer-term conflict management. There is not a single case of peaceful democratization where the minority community was excluded from representation.

The full participation of minorities in politics does not necessarily mean veto power, nor does it imply that minority MPs are the only politicians capable of protecting and advancing the dignity and political interests of marginalized groups. But a progressive democracy which values inclusion is characterized by a situation where members of minority groups can run for office, have a fair chance of winning, and then have a voice in national, regional and locally elected government. Having representatives of one's own group in parliament is not the end of political involvement, but it is the beginning.

Perhaps of most importance, the inclusion of both majorities and minorities within national parliaments can reduce group alienation and violence in those divided societies where politics is often viewed as a win-or-lose game. Many peace settlements over the past 25 years have revolved around inclusive electoral systems or reserved seats for communal groups as part of broader power-sharing constructs. There is a debate about how best to include minority MPs. Should systems be designed so that minorities can be elected through 'usual channels' or are special affirmative action measures needed, like quotas or special appointments? Furthermore, is it better when minority MPs represent 'minority parties' that are rooted in an ethnic community, or should they be integrated into the 'mainstream' parties, which may be ideologically driven or dominated by majority communal groups. This analysis refrains from delving too deeply into that debate and focuses on the first part of the question: exactly how many MPs in the parliaments of the world are from minority communities and what explains their election?

Minority MPs: a league table
The league table shown in Table 2, Reference section (pp. 124–6) is the product of detailed research on the presence of minority MPs in national legislatures around the world. Such comparative data has not been published before and

the 50 cases shown represent approximately a quarter of all countries; we have included both democracies and non-democracies, rich and poor countries, and legislatures from all continents.

Just under half, or 23 of the nation-states, over-represent their minorities when seat share is compared to population share, while the remaining 27 cases, on average, under-represent minority groups. The table details 115 distinct minority groups in the 50 countries: 54 are over-represented in their legislatures while 59 are under-represented. A few minority groups have MPs in legislatures in numbers well above what their population share would suggest. Most notable are Zanzibaris in Tanzania, whites in South Africa, Maronites in Lebanon, Croats in Bosnia and Herzegovina, Walloons in Belgium, Sunnis in Iraq and Herero in Namibia. Sometimes minorities achieve significant representation because their members vote in higher numbers than other groups, but, more often, the 'over-representation' is a product of special mechanisms. In contrast, Russian speakers in Latvia and Estonia, Serbs in Montenegro, Albanians in Macedonia, Bosniaks in Bosnia and Herzegovina, Arabs in Israel and Catalans in Spain are all significantly under-represented.

The top of the league table is something of a surprise. No single type of country consistently over-represents minority populations. The top 10 most 'inclusive' legislatures in the world are found in Africa, Europe, Oceania, North America and the Middle East. Some are peaceful, wealthy, Western democracies, while others are poor, democratically weak, and wrestling with ethnic divisions which still turn violent. The strands that unite the countries that over-represent their minority communities are four-fold: first, there are post-conflict democracies where minority inclusion was a core plank of the power-sharing settlement which brought about an end to civil war and the beginnings of multi-party democracy – e.g. Bosnia and Herzegovina, Lebanon and South Africa. Second, there are nation-states that entrenched power-sharing democracy over a century ago and, while the pressures for minority inclusion may have ebbed over time, the norm of inclusion has remained strong – e.g. Belgium and Switzerland. Third, there are cases which do well on the inclusion of minorities in their parliaments because significant elements of society and party politics are sensitive to minority issues and value minority candidates – e.g. Canada, Finland, the Netherlands and New Zealand. Last, there are countries where the very geographical concentration of a minority group allows such groups to gain significant representation in their national legislatures – e.g. Kiribati, Sri Lanka and Tanzania.

Interestingly, the three top cases are all in sub-Saharan Africa: Namibia, South Africa and Tanzania. Why should these new and sometimes troubled states produce parliaments that are so inclusive of their many minorities? The South African parliament is the most ethnically representative of any democratic legislature in the world. For the reasons discussed below, the promotion of multi-ethnic parties and the deliberate 'over-representation' of minorities was the watchword of the first decade of democracy in South Africa. The same has been true in Namibia, where the liberation movement, the South West Africa People's Organization (SWAPO), while being rooted in the Ovambo majority, sought to present itself as a catch-all party, similar to the African National Congress (ANC) in South Africa or the Congress Party of India. In the current Namibian National Assembly 10 distinct ethnic groups are represented and the majority Ovambo group (representing 60 per cent of the population) only have 50 per cent of the seats. It is true that the Congress of Democrats, Democratic Turnhalle Alliance of Namibia, Monitor Action Group, National Unity Democratic Organisation, Republican Party and United Democratic Front opposition parties have non-Ovambo (bar one) MPs, but SWAPO has two Baster, four Caprivian, two Damara, four Herero, six Kavango, five Nama, three white, a coloured and a San representative. Tanzania's high spot in the table is a result of the over-representation of the island of Zanzibar in their National Assembly.

South Africa is an interesting case study of the positive good of including minorities in governance over and above their population size. Post-apartheid South Africa has consistently done well on indicators of minority representation as a result of two pressures towards accommodation. First, the post-apartheid peace settlement of 1994 (and permanent Constitution of 1996) rested upon a universally accepted principle of multi-ethnic inclusion in the new politics of the nation. A principle beyond that of mere equality, which emphasized the very opposite of the former

Table 1 Cabinet ministers in South Africa

		Black	White	Coloured	Indian
1994	Ministers	52%	26%	7%	15%
	Ministers and Deputies	51%	28%	5%	15%
1999	Ministers	76%	7%	3%	14%
	Ministers and Deputies	76%	9%	2%	12%
2006	Ministers	81%	11%	4%	4%
	Ministers and Deputies	68%	18%	4%	8%
Population		74%	14%	8%	2%

apartheid laws, that is, the new South African government would deliberately reach out to minorities to visibly demonstrate their full role in governance. Second, it quickly became apparent that, to be successful, any Xhosa party had to reach out to non-Xhosa, a Zulu party would atrophy if Zulu nationalism remained its *raison d'être*, and white parties could only gain leverage if they became multi-ethnic vehicles. Thus, the ANC under Nelson Mandela deliberately placed coloureds, Indians, whites and Zulus high up on its lists of candidates in 1994 and 1999. This diversity goes beyond the simple black–white divide. As a 'catch-all' national movement, the ANC seeks to exist in a universe beyond the Xhosa community which has historically dominated its leadership. It strives to attract the votes of Ndebele, Pedi, Sotho, Tswana, Venda, along with Zulu in KwaZulu, coloureds in the Cape, and English- and Afrikaans-speaking whites throughout the country. These appeals are often based on policy promises, but just as much on having senior 'ethnic' politicians high up on the party lists. The same has been true for the opposition – the white-dominated Democratic Alliance places non-white leaders in visible positions – and was even true for the now defunct National Party, which, in its failure to attract sufficient non-white leaders and voters, was ultimately subsumed into the ANC in the most remarkable power-shift between two long opposed movements in the history of modern politics. While

the level of minority over-representation has declined under Thabo Mbeki, it still exists in 2006. Nevertheless, consolidating democracy and stability will rest upon continuing this ethos of minority inclusion and respect.

At the executive level, South Africans have also felt that it is important to visibly include minorities. As Table 1 shows, white and Indian South Africans were dramatically 'over-represented' in the first decade of democratic governance under Presidents Nelson Mandela and Thabo Mbeki. The over-representation of whites and Indians was most pronounced in 1994 and 1999, but when ministers and their deputies are taken together it remains to this day.

The deliberate reaching out to smaller minority groups and institutions, designed to ensure the widest inclusion possible, was particularly key in 1994, when South Africa made its first tentative steps towards a multi-party electoral democracy. Two very small parties gained representation in the first National Assembly (the Freedom Front and Pan-Africanist Congress of Azania), facilitating conflict resolution by democratic rather than violent means. Although the Afrikaner Freedom Front only won nine (or 2 per cent) of the seats, the importance of their inclusion in democratic structures was disproportionate to their numbers. General Constand Viljoen's Freedom Front represented a volatile Afrikaner constituency that could easily have fallen into the hands of white supremacist demagogues such as Eugene

Terre'blanche had its representatives been shut out of the political process. As it was, Viljoen, as former head of the South African Army, became chair of the National Assembly's Defence Select Committee and the paramilitary Afrikaner resistance faded away.

Representing a very different place and time, the inclusion of minority politicians in Canada today is a second positive example of how majority politics can provide a space to hear and reassure minority communities. Electoral system specialists would expect the First Past the Post system of elections in Canada to provide a high hurdle to the election of non-white, non-majority MPs, but Canadian parties and voters have managed to circumvent the majoritarianism of their Anglo election system to produce a parliament which includes, and over-represents, Asians, Canadians of African extraction and Francophone Canadians. Inuits are under-represented in the House of Commons but they have some access to self-governance through the semi-autonomous province of Nunavut.

The inclusion of French-Canadian politicians in large numbers is perhaps unsurprising considering the powerful leverage Quebec has long had over national Canadian politics, but much smaller minorities are also heard in parliament. There are 21 MPs from minority backgrounds in addition to the French-speaking MPs – ten of South Asian extraction, five Chinese, four African or Afro-Caribbean, one Middle Eastern and one Canadian Inuit. Importantly, these minority MPs are not clustered in 'ethnic' political parties. Twelve are in the opposition Liberal Party, six in the governing Conservative party, two in the Bloc Québécois and one in the New Democratic Party. The spread of minority MPs across parties is mirrored in the Netherlands, where the 15 MPs of African, Afro-Caribbean, Iranian, Moroccan or Turkish background are split between Christian Democratic Appeal (4), Democrats 66 (1), Green Left (4), Labour Party (3), List Pym Fortuyn (1) and Peoples Party for Freedom and Democracy (2). While the Netherlands demonstrates the progress that can be made when parties and voters promote multi-ethnicity, the country also illustrates the reality that, even in the most progressive polities, issues of minority rights and respect can still be problematic and vulnerable to anti-immigration elements of society.

The bottom of the league table (pp. 124–6) is also a jumble of very different countries. Half of the bottom 10 are Central European/Baltic states that

democratized in the early 1990s and, in those cases, the under-representation is focused on Albanian, Russian or Serb minority communities. Nevertheless, only in Montenegro is the Serbian community assessed by MRG as being significantly 'under threat'. Outside Central Europe, the most under-represented minorities are found in Brazil, Israel, Spain and the United States. All 10 cases represent very different levels of human development, wealth and democracy.

One of the most important cases that scores poorly on the indicator of minority inclusion in parliament is Afghanistan. On one level we see a high degree of diversity in the new Afghan Wolesi Jirga: there are 30 Hazaras, 53 Tajiks, 20 Uzbeks and 28 others, representing minority communities. There are significant 'minority' leaders in parliament and government. Yunus Qanooni (a Tajik) is Speaker of the Wolesi Jirga, Mohammed Mohaqeq (a Hazara) received the most votes of any candidates in Kabul, and Rashid Dostom (an Uzbek) is Chief of Staff of the Afghan National Army. Ten seats are reserved in the Assembly for the nomadic Kuchi population. President Karzai's cabinet is also diverse, and minority MPs can be found on both the pro-government and opposition benches, but, as the league table (pp. 124–6), each of the four main minority groups is under-represented in the legislature, while the largest group, the Pashtuns, is over-represented. This is a sensitive political issue as Tajiks from the Northern Alliance and Uzbeks from the north feel increasingly marginalized by what they term the 'Pashtun mafia' which surrounds President Karzai.

What explains levels of minority representation?

A number of variables might be expected to influence the level of minority representation in national legislatures (Table 3, Reference section, pp. 128–9).

So what explains minority inclusion in legislative politics: region, electoral system, development or level of democracy? Regionally we see that the six cases from Africa (Malawi, Namibia, South Africa, Tanzania, Zambia and Zimbabwe) on average over-represent their minority groups, but a caution should be noted. First, these results are driven by the impressive minority inclusion of Namibia, South Africa and Tanzania, which may not be replicated in

Table 2 Minority representation by region

	Africa	Middle East	Western Europe	Oceania	North America	Asia	C-East Europe	Latin America
No. over	6	2	6	3	1	1	4	0
No. under	0	1	6	3	2	4	10	1
Average	1.8	0.3	0.3	-0.2	-0.7	-1.2	-1.3	-3.28

Table 3 Does adequate representation depend on reserved seats for minorities?

	Reserved seats	No reserved seats
Cases over-represented	6	17
Cases under-represented	6	21

Table 4 Minority representation and electoral system

	BV	MMP	FPTP	TRS	List PR	STV	AV	PAR	SNTV
Average	0.5	0.2	-0.04	-0.3	-0.5	-0.5	-0.9	-1.3	-3.2
No. cases	2	3	11	2	26	1	3	1	1

Table 5 Minority representation by level of democracy

Free	-0.7	35
Partly free	0.2	10
Not free	-0.3	4

other African states, and Malawi, Zambia and Zimbabwe have positive scores because one or two Asians or whites make it into their parliaments. The Middle East scores well because of Lebanon and Iraq, but clearly neither case is a poster child for inter-ethnic harmony. The picture is more mixed in Western Europe, Oceania and North America, and decidedly negative in Asia and Central and Eastern Europe, and Latin America (see Table 2).

Many groups have called for electoral system reforms to ensure and encourage minority access to elected office, but, while such democratic changes may help, the data suggest that electoral system design only has a limited role in promoting minority representation. Half of the countries that reserve seats for minorities end up over-representing them, while the other half under-represent (see Table 3). Just over half the countries that do not have reserved seats under-represent their minorities, but the other half manage to over-represent despite not having any special mechanisms.

When it comes to electoral system, we can discern patterns in the data but the results are again surprising in certain respects (see Table 4). The five countries that use the Block Vote and Mixed Member Proportional systems do best at including minorities, but Lebanon and New Zealand drive those high figures. Interestingly, First Past the Post systems, long criticized for providing hurdles to minority representation, do better than List proportional systems. But again the average scores can be misleading as seven of the top ten states in the league table use List PR election systems. Overall, none of the electoral system 'families', when combined, produce more minority members than their population share. Majoritarian systems (First Past the Post, the Block Vote, Two-Round Systems, and the Alternative Vote) score -0.1, proportional systems (List PR, Mixed Member Proportional and the Single Transferable Vote) -0.4, and semi-proportional systems (Parallel Systems and the Single Non-transferable Vote) -2.2.

Perhaps most surprising is the finding that the nation-states least able to demonstrate minority inclusion are, on average, the most democratic. The 35 cases ranked as 'free' democracies by the Freedom in the World survey produced by Freedom House are the least likely to fully represent their minorities, while the 10 cases ranked as 'partly free' on average marginally over-represent minorities in their legislatures (see Table 5).

As noted earlier, the inclusion of some minority MPs within a national legislature is only the first step towards minority protection. One could imagine a situation where a few token minority MPs were elected (or appointed), but minority rights remained severely curtailed. So is there a relationship between the number of minority representatives in parliament and the degree of threat these minority groups live under? Compare the top 20 countries which represent minorities best in their national legislatures (Table 2, Reference Section, pp.124–6) and MRG's People Under Threat (Table 1, Reference Section, pp.118–123). While overall, the countries which represent minorities best, are generally those where minorities are not most at risk, the appearance of Iraq at No 2 (PUT), Bosnia at No 20 (PUT), and Sri Lanka at No 22 (PUT) illustrates that sometimes minorities can gain significant political representation, but still be marginalized from real decision-making influence, and live under significant challenges to their security.

How is minority inclusion best achieved?

The findings outlined in this research suggest that political designs matter at the margins but, ultimately, minorities have access to elected office if the society is open to minority inclusion, or power-sharing arrangements dictate 'fair shares' in parliament for majority and minority groups. If minority MPs are deemed to be of value to voters or political elites then the barriers of exclusionary election systems, under-development and authoritarianism will be navigated.

Nevertheless, all else being equal, there are some lessons to be noted. First, much of the progress on issues of minority inclusion and representation has occurred not in the established democracies of Europe and North America but in new electoral regimes in Africa, the Middle East and the South Pacific. Second, even when minorities do gain representation in national parliaments they are often discriminated against, face threats to their integrity and are marginalized from real power. Last, the actual method and scope of minority inclusion needs to be crafted to fit the needs of the given country. Some states may do better with reserved seats or autonomous self-governing assemblies, while others will require incentives for minority MPs to be involved in 'mainstream' parties and have a guarantee of both legislative and executive representation. The key is to ensure both visibility and voice: to have minorities in parliament and enable them to impact policies that affect not only their communal affairs but the well-being of society as a whole. ■

Minority Protection in Europe: What about Effective Participation?

Kristin Henrard

Although minority protection has come mor...
forefront since the 1990s, both at the inte...
level and at national level, many inadeq...
remain, not only regarding the standa...
themselves, but also and especially c...
actual implementation and enforc...
Nevertheless, several positive de...
and should be highlighted.

When discussing minori...
important to realize that...
rights of 'persons belor...
specific rights). Inde...
the prohibition of...
with general hur...
person), shoul...

There is a...
minority...
(minori...
on th...
con...
d...

...for persons
...d not be
..., education, etc.
...s to formal
...cy does not seem to
...iorities because it does
...nces in circumstances,
...ty with a separate identity
...iold on to this minority
ia...   of substantive equality can be
helpfu...   .e this understanding of equality
accepts that ...ential treatment (formally unequal
treatment) or special rights might be necessary to
reach real, genuine equality. To the extent that the
interpretation of general human rights is not
(sufficiently) suffused by substantive equality
considerations and does not provide protection for
the right to identity of minorities, the minority-
specific standards form a necessary complement.

The focus of this annual report, and of this
article, is on the participation of minorities. The
concept 'participation' needs clarification. It seems
obvious that it can be interpreted broadly. In this
article, the central importance of participation is
underlined, and a generous approach is adopted as
to the potential reach of the concept.

The other central concept in this article, namely
'minority', also does not have a generally agreed

...particularly controversial
...it persons belonging to
...e the nationality of the
...able to avail
...rity protection. A
...ether (and to what
...qualify as minorities.
...e two central concepts of
...sed; this is followed by a
...most relevant developments in
...urope, the Organization for
...Cooperation in Europe (OSCE) and
...ropean Union (EU). An overview is then
...n of recurring problems in several European
...ates, after which some concluding observations are
made about the actual and potential protection of
minorities in Europe.

What do we mean by 'minority' and 'participation'?

Although there is no set legal definition of the
term 'minority', there is broad agreement about
certain requirements: that minorities should have
stable ethnic, religious or linguistic characteristics
that are different from those of the rest of the
population, a numerical minority position, non-
dominance and the wish to preserve their own,
separate cultural identity.

However, it is important to note that, under
international legal norms, states do not explicitly
have the right to decide which groups count as
minorities. This point was underlined by the United
Nations (UN) Human Rights Committee, the body
tasked with monitoring the International Covenant
on Civil and Political Rights (ICCPR). In its
General Comment on Article 27, the Human
Rights Committee stated that individuals need not
be citizens of the state to have minority rights
protection. Although not legally binding, the
Committee's Comments are widely seen as
authoritative statements on the scope of ICCPR.

The Human Rights Committee position,
however, is in conflict with the position traditionally
adopted by states, which have often been adamant
about the need for persons belonging to minorities
to have the nationality of the country of residence.
This requirement is increasingly criticized for the
following reasons. Nationality legislation can all too
easily be manipulated by the public authorities.
Especially in cases of state succession and change of

frontiers, such a requirement seems problematic, as is clearly apparent in the Baltic states. Nationality is also difficult to satisfy for nomadic groups. Finally, and especially in countries where it is difficult to acquire nationality, it may seem inappropriate to exclude certain groups that have lived in the country for decades or even generations. Where to draw the line will ultimately be an arbitrary decision. Hence it seems more appropriate not to focus on nationality or immigrant status as such, but rather to adopt a more pragmatic attitude, taking into account all the relevant circumstances and deciding on a case-by-case basis whether a particular group can enjoy minority rights.

Slowly but surely, the tide seems to be turning as states increasingly, if only *de facto*, treat immigrant groups as minorities. It is striking that a nationality requirement does not feature in the majority of the declarations of contracting states to the 1995 Framework Convention for the Protection of National Minorities (FCNM), the only legally binding document that is exclusively devoted to the protection of minorities. Furthermore, the Advisory Committee supervising the implementation of the FCNM clearly adopted an inclusive approach, urging states to consider whether they cannot expand the reach of the Convention on an article-by-article basis with respect to immigrant groups as well.

Most minority rights provisions contain escape clauses or conditional clauses, like 'where appropriate', 'when necessary', etc., which could easily be used by contracting states to avoid their obligations. However, the positive side to such standards is their inherent flexibility, which allows them to cater for the tremendous diversity of minority situations. Indeed, not all groups qualifying as minorities should necessarily have equally strong rights. In this respect, some have advocated a 'sliding-scale' approach, especially in relation to rights that would impose financial burdens on the public authorities. Following this approach, the state would have more far-reaching obligations towards minority groups of a greater size (and a higher level of territorial concentration). Likewise, states would have less far-reaching obligations in relation to newly immigrated groups (often called 'new' minorities, as opposed to the traditional, autochthonous minorities). At the same time, clearly it is essential that the exercise of this state discretion should be suitably monitored so as to ensure that states do not abuse it.

International human rights law provides for the right to participation – for example Article 25 of ICCPR holds that: 'every citizen shall have the right and the opportunity ... without unreasonable restrictions to ... take part in the conduct of public affairs'. This has subsequently been taken up in minority-specific instruments: Article 2, paragraphs 2 and 3 of the UN Declaration on the Rights of Persons belonging to National or Ethnic, Religious and Linguistic Minorities (UNDM; stipulating respectively the right to participation in the cultural, religious, social, economic and public spheres of life and the right to participate in decisions concerning the minority to which they belong), and Article 15 of the FCNM (enshrining the right to effective participation in cultural, social and economic life, and in public affairs, in particular those affecting them). But the difficulty is that there is no legal definition of what the concept of 'participation' entails.

It is generally agreed that, potentially, the concept has a very broad reach. The High Commissioner on National Minorities (HCNM) has instigated and endorsed in 1999 the Lund Recommendations on the Effective Participation of National Minorities in Public Life. These Recommendations are made by independent experts and hence are not legally binding. Nevertheless, as they are rooted in minority rights and other standards generally applicable in the situations in which the HCNM is involved, they cannot be ignored. Two major dimensions of participation are distinguished in the Recommendations, namely 'participation in decision-making' and 'self-governance'. The former is actually mostly concerned with issues of 'representation' in the broad sense, as it addresses not only representation in parliament (e.g. reserved seats for minority groups) and government/executive bodies, but also members of minorities in the civil service, the police and the judiciary, and even deals with the establishment of advisory bodies and other consultation mechanisms. It also deals with election systems (including references to forms of preference voting and lower numerical thresholds for representation in the legislature for minority political parties).

It should be emphasized, though, that while the political dimension of participation traditionally attracts most attention, there are also important economic, social and cultural dimensions to participation. In regard to economic participation, there is the issue of access to employment. Unemployment is a serious problem for many persons belonging to minorities, especially the 'new' minorities and the Roma.

In this regard, but also more generally, it is important to underline the inherent link between adequate participation and the prohibition of discrimination. It can indeed be argued that full participation of minorities would only be possible when there is no discrimination against persons belonging to minorities. There is a growing acknowledgement of the phenomenon of indirect discrimination, the prohibition of which targets rules that are apparently neutral but which have a disproportionate negative impact on particular groups (without justification). A good example would be the competence in language required in relation to standing for elections or for access to jobs, as is the case in Latvia and Estonia. Requirements in terms of the official language of the state are inherently more difficult to fulfil for foreigners. Insofar as these requirements would not be proportionate in relation to the position concerned, they would be indirectly discriminatory (and thus prohibited).

Indirect discrimination is closely related to the understanding that the prohibition of discrimination also requires differential treatment of substantively different situations. This, in turn, appears inherently linked to a duty to reasonably accommodate different identities and lifestyles, which is slowly gaining ground. Arguably this *could* have repercussions for regulations on the wearing of the headscarf in education and employment, special food, special rules in relation to festive days of minority religions, special attention to the lifestyle of nomadic groups and the like (see, for example, the Recommendations on Policing in Multi-Ethnic Societies endorsed by the HCNM).

Of course, the word 'reasonably' clearly indicates that this duty to accommodate would not be an absolute, unlimited duty. This is reflected in the practice of the Commission on Equal Treatment of the Netherlands. While that Commission tends to qualify prohibitions to wear the headscarf in employment and education as violations of the General Equal Treatment Act, because they would

amount to indirect discrimination on the basis of religion, it often allows prohibitions on the *nikaab* and the *burka*, because, in the Commission's view, there would be reasonable justifications for these prohibitions.

The concept 'participation' has a very broad reach indeed. It would be difficult to deny that the absence of reasonable accommodation of differences would not hamper the full and genuine participation of the persons concerned. Furthermore, full participation would also send important symbolic messages about inclusion, essential for an optimal integration. In the words of the previous HCNM, Max van der Stoel: 'participation has a broader connotation, namely that minorities feel that they are active and equal members of the state' (Speech by the OSCE High Commissioner on National Minorities at a conference in Slovenia, February 2001).

Minority protection in Europe
Council of Europe
It has often been pointed out that, while effective protection against discrimination and of general human rights is very important for minorities, the case law of the European Court of Human Rights, supervising the European Convention on Human Rights (ECHR) is in many respects inadequate.

The Court has often been criticized for its apparent reluctance to conclude that violations of the prohibition against discrimination have occurred. While this is still a problematic area, there have been some important developments. The cases of *Nachova v. Bulgaria* (26 February 2004, partially confirmed by the Grand Chamber of the Court on 6 July 2005, concerning the killings of two Roma by military police) and *Timishev v. Russia* (13 December 2005, concerning the refusal to allow a Chechen person to enter another republic of Russia) clearly indicate that the Court is becoming more vigilant in relation to alleged racial discrimination. In the latter case, the Court explicitly held that 'no difference in treatment which is based exclusively or to a decisive extent on a person's ethnic origin is capable of being objectively justified in a contemporary democratic society built on the principles of pluralism and respect for different cultures' (para. 58). As both cases concern minorities, they confirm the special importance of the prohibition of discrimination for minorities.

In *Thlimmenos v. Greece* (6 April 2000) the Court had made a very important pronouncement on the prohibition of discrimination, which implied a crucial opening towards substantive equality. The Court underlined in its judgment that the prohibition of discrimination can also be violated when states fail to treat differently persons in substantively different situations (without justification). In other words, the prohibition of discrimination gives rise to a duty to adopt differential measures in certain circumstances. This clearly holds the promise of a duty to adopt minority-specific measures in order to reasonably accommodate their different identities and lifestyles. This could possibly concern regulations to reasonably accommodate persons belonging to minority religions and their specific needs as to timing of work, dress code and the like. The link between these measures and full and effective participation has already been made. However, the subsequent case law has been rather modest and has not (yet) ventured along this path.

The case law of the Court so far has revealed that it struggles with the concept of indirect discrimination. The latest case in which this was particularly visible and detrimental for minorities was *D.H. et al. v. Czech Republic* (7 February 2006). Despite the convincing statistical evidence that Roma children were disproportionately sidelined to schools for mentally retarded children, the Court failed to find a violation of the prohibition of discrimination.

The ECHR is not explicitly geared towards the protection and promotion of minority identity. However, a lot depends on the interpretation of concepts that are in themselves vague and open-ended. A good example is *Chapman v. UK* (18 January 2001), where the Court for the first time acknowledged that the right to respect for private life, family life and home actually enshrines a right to a traditional way of life, and that states have positive obligations to facilitate the minority way of life. However, states have broad margins of discretion in this respect and *de facto* protection still remains low.

An interesting case in relation to political participation, of special relevance for linguistic minorities, is *Podkolzina v. Latvia* (9 April 2002). This concerned a person of Russian ethnicity who was ultimately barred from standing for election because she did not have the required language proficiency in Latvian. The Court found it legitimate for a state to set linguistic requirements for candidates for parliament. It concluded that there was a violation of the Podkolzina's 'election right', not because the content of the measure – the linguistic requirement itself – was disproportionate, but because of the way it was administered *in casu*. Even though it would have been welcome if the Court had explicitly indicated that there are also limits on what exactly can be required (content of the measure) in this respect, this judgment in any event sends a signal to states that they do not have unlimited discretion in the way in which they impose linguistic requirements for certain functions. This could be an indication that the Court, in future, might be more attentive to protecting linguistic minorities more generally.

Since the 1990s there has been long line of case law in which the Court emphasizes that states are not allowed to limit the freedom of association of members of minorities merely because the association would aim to promote the culture of a minority. However, the judgment in *Gorzelik and others v. Poland* (20 December 2001, confirmed by the Grand Chamber of the Court on 17 February 2004; on the refusal to register an association under the name 'Union of People of Silesian Nationality') seems to deviate from this case law. While there are no clear context-specific variables that explain the a-typical outcome in *Gorzelik*, the combination of two areas in which states are accorded a broad margin of appreciation, namely the identification of minorities and electoral matters, could explain this particular outcome. It should in any event be underlined that, in subsequent case law, the Court has returned to its protective stance.

The Court traditionally has provided ample protection to religious minorities in terms of freedom of religion, inter alia by underscoring states' duty to protect and promote religious tolerance and pluralism. However, in a country like Turkey, where the great majority of people are Muslim, where there is a history of a sensitive, fragile relation between religions and state, and a perceived danger of religiously inspired movements/political parties taking over, the supervisory organs of the ECHR seem willing to accept considerable limitations to the freedom to manifest one's religion (by wearing the headscarf). The case that received most critical attention in this respect was *Leyla Sahin v. Turkey*. According to the Court (10 November 2005, confirmed by the Grand Chamber on 29 June 2004), the prohibition on wearing the veil in a state university in Turkey did not amount to a violation of the freedom to manifest one's religion (under Article 9 of the ECHR). It is to be hoped that the Court will be equally context sensitive if a case comes before it from a Muslim girl faced with a similar prohibition in a country without this specific historical background, where Muslims are not in the majority and where the danger of pressurizing others would not be present.

The preceding overview arguably hints at a rather ambivalent picture with regard to the contribution of individual human rights to minority protection. Remarkable advances at the theoretical level in relation to embracing both substantive equality considerations and the right to identity of minorities, are not always matched by equally progressive, minority-sensitive applications in concrete cases. Furthermore, in certain areas where the Court has traditionally realized a meaningful level of minority protection, decisions in a few recent cases have gone against this trend and hence threaten to question this traditionally minority-sensitive case law.

Nevertheless, it should be emphasized, the case law clearly reveals tremendous *potential* to provide enhanced levels of minority protection on the basis of general human rights and the prohibition of discrimination. It is to be hoped that the Court will, in the future, actually realize this potential. Since the judgments of the Court are legally binding for the states against which they are pronounced, they do tend to lead to changes in the law and practice of these states (and also of other states).

As was pointed out above, the FCNM has an explicit minority focus. Considering the central importance of substantive equality and the right to a minority identity for mechanisms of minority protection, it should not come as a surprise that this Convention has these as guiding principles. Article 15 explicitly addresses the effective participation of persons belonging to national minorities in cultural, social and economic life, and in public affairs.

It is the practice of the supervisory mechanism in terms of Article 15 that will be focused upon here. However, it should be acknowledged that some issues of relevance to full participation are focused upon in other articles of the FCNM and hence no longer attract attention in terms of Article 15. This does not mean, though, that these issues would not be considered as important or relevant for participation purposes. A good example here would be rules on the use of a minority language in communication with public authorities, and rules on language in education. Similarly, the practice of some states of assigning Roma children to special schools for mentally retarded children is problematic in view of the requirement of equal access to education (Article 12(3) and Article 4 on equal treatment).

Linguistic requirements to stand for elections are addressed in terms of Article 15, and the same can be said about such requirements in relation to access to employment. Such requirements should not be too rigid or demanding, so as to prevent a negative impact on effective participation of minorities.

Issues pertaining to religious accommodation do not attract much attention, either in the text of the FCNM or in the supervisory practice. Participation of religious groups is definitely considered but not (so far) in terms of duties to reasonably accommodate the specific needs of religious minorities.

Notwithstanding the fact that the FCNM stipulates that the Committee of Ministers of the Council of Europe has the final responsibility for the supervision of the Convention, the importance of the opinions of the independent expert body, the Advisory Committee (AC) is now undisputed. Indeed, the Committee of Ministers has begun to follow the opinions of the AC, and even refers back to them for further detail in its Resolutions. Hence, the focus of this analysis will be on the opinions of the AC. One general remark that needs to be made is that the supervision by the AC has revealed that the discretion of contracting states to the FCNM is not as boundless as it may seem at first sight.

The AC has recently added another tool to its supervisory practice: the adoption of thematic reports reflecting and synthesizing its experience and views on specific thematic issues. The first report was adopted in March 2006 and is entitled *Commentary on Education under the Framework Convention for the Protection of National Minorities*. A wealth of issues is addressed in this report, as is evidenced by the following description:

'the Commentary recognizes that the Framework Convention is of relevance not only in guaranteeing the rights of persons belonging to minorities to good quality, free primary education as well as general and equal access to secondary education (right to education) but also in setting standards on how such education should be shaped in terms of content as well as form (rights in education) in order to facilitate the development of the abilities and personality of the child, guarantee child safety and accommodate the linguistic, religious, philosophical aspirations of pupils and their parents'. (Commentary on Education under the FCNM, p. 4)

It should be highlighted that the AC is currently working on a Commentary on political participation.

When reading through the opinions of the AC, its emphasis on the need to consult and to maintain a dialogue with minorities on all the issues addressed in the FCNM is hard to miss. The central importance of consultation and even involvement of minorities in relation to policies of (direct or indirect) relevance to them, can be explained by its double effect of enhancing integration (inclusion) of minorities while strengthening their identity. It seems obvious that when minority groups are allowed a say in the construction and implementation of policies and programmes concerning them, this is bound to improve the quality, efficiency and overall impact of the latter.

The AC encourages states not only to go beyond mere *ad hoc* consultation and to make dialogue a regular, preferably institutionalized feature, but also makes suggestions on how this participation can be more 'effective'. The AC shows itself to be increasingly demanding about the effectiveness of participation, in the sense that it should be meaningful, which implies that the ideas of minorities are to be taken seriously. The AC appears to consider consultation as the bare minimum and often goes beyond mere consultation, urging states to coordinate and cooperate on minority policies with the minorities concerned. 'Cooperation' seems to indicate that the minorities' opinions should be reflected in the actual outcome.

While this consultation theme is omni-present, it should be highlighted that the AC clearly focuses on the public affairs component in Article 15. Participation in cultural, social and economic life is given significantly less attention. The AC is nevertheless particularly attentive towards the problems of economic exclusion of the Roma in virtually all contracting states, while also urging some states to address shortcomings in the participation of other minorities in economic life. Increasingly, the AC seems to address the social situation of Roma as well, looking at their problems with regard to access to housing and health care, as well as the resulting shortcomings in their living conditions.

It has already been emphasized that the AC is critical about language requirements that do not seem necessary in order to work in particular functions or deliver certain services. Nevertheless, it seems that the AC could expand its review in terms of the effective participation of minorities in economic, social and cultural life.

With regard to the public affairs component, it is noteworthy that the AC regularly starts by noting that minorities are not, or not sufficiently, present in parliament (or other elected bodies), and encourages authorities to examine thoroughly all the barriers that might hinder minority representation in political life and to develop mechanisms to redress this situation, particularly in relation to small and scattered minorities. More recently, the AC has expressed concern about insufficient representation of minorities' interests in the decision-making process. The AC, furthermore, does not limit its review to elected and executive bodies, but also often speaks out against low levels of minority members in the judiciary, the civil service, the police, the army and the prison service. In relation to employment in the civil service, the AC expresses (again) concern about too-demanding linguistic requirements.

Finally, the AC addresses an area that is closely connected to the sovereignty of states and for which states have generally not been willing to accept far-reaching international commitments, namely citizenship legislation. It is obvious that citizenship is still a requirement for the exercise of (most) electoral rights and hence is essential for political participation. The central importance of the prohibition of discrimination makes it possible for the AC to point out that governments should make sure that legislation on citizenship is applied fairly and in a non-discriminatory fashion. According to the AC, the presence of large numbers of non-citizens would cast doubts in this respect, particularly in cases of the break-up of states and state succession.

It may be obvious that, in terms of the FCNM, the contracting parties are continuously invited and even urged to improve the full and effective participation of persons belonging to national minorities. Even though the outcome of this supervisory process is not legally binding, the second round of monitoring has clearly revealed high levels of compliance with the Recommendations. It is to be welcomed that the contracting states recognize its authority as in fact coming from the bodies that are responsible for the supervision of its implementation by the states.

OSCE

The activities of the OSCE in relation to minorities are not limited to those of the High Commissioner on National Minorities, as can be witnessed, inter alia, from the existence of the Roma Contact Point. Within the OSCE more generally there has been heightened attention to the plight of the Roma across the participating states. This led in 2003 to the adoption of the *Action Plan on Improving the Situation of Roma and Sinti in the OSCE Area.* However, in view of space limitations, it seems appropriate to focus on the HCNM because of its explicit focus on national minorities (in general).

It would be difficult to capture comprehensively the multiple activities of the HCNM in relation to national minorities. The country-specific work of the HCNM continues to underline the importance of comprehensive integration strategies, entailing special attention to the effective participation of persons belonging to national minorities, and especially the Roma. Themes that are taken up and criticized are the under-representation of Roma in the legislative bodies, and the lack of consultation of Roma when policies on Roma are being developed.

In addition to the country-specific work and ensuing recommendations, the HCNM has been involved (since 1995) in the elaboration of more thematic recommendations, concerning issues that recur in virtually all minority situations. The HCNM does not have a mandate of standard-setting, but has adopted a practice of bringing together international experts to draw up Recommendation on such themes, which he

subsequently endorses. These Recommendations are based on the existing standards but are more detailed, and hence provide important additional guidance. In relation to participation, the Lund Recommendations on the Effective Participation of National Minorities (1999) should of course be highlighted. Nevertheless, the earlier Recommendations on Education Rights (1996) and Language Rights (1998) also concern issues with important repercussions for the full participation of minorities. Similarly, it can be remarked that the *Guidelines on the Use of Minority Languages in the Broadcast Media* (2003), and their goal of equal access to mainstream public media, are essential for optimal integration and adequate participation of minorities.

The year 2006 witnessed the adoption of a new set of recommendations, namely on Policing in Multi-ethnic Societies. Various themes addressed in these Recommendations are very important for a full participation of minorities in society. The need for an equitable representation of minorities within the police force, at all levels in the hierarchy, is obviously relevant. It is not difficult to see that minorities will feel more 'included' when members of their group are part of the police force. Other themes that are important in this respect concern the way in which the police engage with ethnic communities and, more generally, the way in which they exercise their functions, including questions of use of force and the need to avoid even the impression of 'ethnic profiling'. The importance of a neutral working environment should not be underestimated either; or, better, a working environment that adequately accommodates the population diversity present in the force. The policing recommendations are particularly innovative because they not only look at linguistic diversity but also at religious diversity. The 'Explanatory Note to the Recommendations' explicitly points out that the working environment should be sensitive to diversity in the needs, customs and religions of different groups (e.g. with regard to matters of dress, diet and religious observances such as prayer and holy days).

In view of these characteristics of the policing recommendations, it is particularly noteworthy that they have been very well received by the OSCE states. While the OSCE may not have the power to adopt legally binding decisions, the documents produced by its institutions and bodies, including the work of the HCNM, do possess considerable *de facto* political authority.

European Union

In relation to the European Union and minority protection, it should first of all be emphasized that the original, and still the main focus of that organization, namely economic integration, lends itself less evidently to the adoption of minority policies. Furthermore, the EU only has those competences that are explicitly attributed to it in the founding treaties and there is no explicit competence concerning minority protection attributed to the EU. This explains why there are no explicit EU standards in relation to minority protection and no explicit demands on the member states to respect minority rights.

Nevertheless, this has not prevented the EU from demanding that third states comply with minority rights standards, which has led to the well-known complaint about double standards. The best-known example is in relation to countries wanting to accede to the EU. The reference to the need to respect and protect minorities in the political Copenhagen Criteria (the requirements that have to be satisfied by candidate countries in order to accede to the EU) has drawn the European Commission into monitoring and evaluating the candidates' progress in relation to minority protection. Since there were no internal EU benchmarks, the annual reports used the standards adopted in the Council of Europe and the OSCE. Arguably, this synergy in the use of standards adds to their strength. Furthermore, the European Commission relied heavily on the information coming from the opinions of the Advisory Committee of the FCNM and the HCNM. Since these sources of information concern independent expert bodies, this reduces (at least to some extent), the danger of politicization of the supervision.

Nevertheless, it cannot be denied that the monitoring exercise revealed a clear hierarchy of minority issues. In the 10 recently acceded countries, two minority groups were consistently stressed, specifically the Russophone minority in Estonia and Latvia and, more generally, the Roma minority. Nevertheless, most of the countries concerned have several other minority groups. In relation to Bulgaria and Romania, this virtually

exclusive focus on the Roma was apparent. While the Roma are undoubtedly the most excluded and disadvantaged minority group in these countries, this hierarchy can (also) be translated in terms of political sensitivities: on the one hand, it is important for the EU to maintain good relations with its most powerful energy supplier, Russia (hence the attention paid to the Russian minority in candidate countries); and, on the other hand, the Roma as a minority group are considerably less politically sensitive in comparison with well organized, politically mobilized and territorially concentrated groups like the Hungarians in Slovakia and Romania. In other words, it is harder for states to comply with political demands for autonomy (or other issues) because of political sensitivities, than it is for them to improve the situation (living conditions, employment, education, etc.) of the Roma.

This political dimension is also visible in the way in which the political criteria are used in the accession monitoring. In relation to the 10 recently acceded countries, there was a clear political determination to proceed with enlargement, which translated itself into the absence of harsh criticisms. Even if some shortcomings were highlighted, the end conclusion remained that the political criteria had been fulfilled.

When reviewing the European Commission reports in relation to the current three candidate countries, Croatia, Macedonia and Turkey, a different overall picture emerges, which can still – to some extent at least – be explained in terms of political considerations. Arguably, the practice in relation to Macedonia is closest to that for the 10 recently acceded countries: the evaluation is quite easy-going and not very detailed. While there are several references to ongoing ethnic tensions, the most sensitive minority, the Albanians, is never mentioned by name.

The 2005 report on Croatia is definitely different in tone; it goes into much more detail and is more critical. The extensive attention paid to issues of political participation of 'minorities' is striking in this report. There is again a focus on the Roma minority but now also on the Serb minority. Apparently, in this case, the EU has less difficulty in addressing 'sensitive' minorities; though it is difficult to deny that the situation in Macedonia is potentially much more explosive than it is in Croatia.

Be that as it may, the accession monitoring in relation to Turkey clearly stands out as being very elaborate, and critical, which is arguably in line with the lack of clear political determination to proceed with the accession of this country. The European Commission is very critical of the Turkish position that the only minorities in Turkey would be non-Muslim minorities. The Commission focuses on several non-religious themes, such as language rights and language in education, and is particularly critical of the treatment of the Kurdish minority. The Roma minority in Turkey is also paid special attention – as are the Muslim minorities, particularly the Alevis.

Notwithstanding the legitimacy problem facing the EU when it is accused of double standards, it should not be forgotten that all member states, old and new, are member states of the OSCE and contracting parties to the ECHR, and that most of the old member states have also ratified the FCNM. The impact of the related supervisory mechanisms should not be underestimated and is conducted by independent bodies.

It is not surprising that it has been remarked that it is difficult to pin down the exact relationship between domestic incentives and EU conditionality, and the conditions and recommendations of the EU, the OSCE and the Council of Europe overlap, making it impossible to separate their respective effects. Furthermore, an empirical study of what happened in relation to minority protection in a selection of recently acceded Central and Eastern Europe countries has revealed that international pressures were important to set the process in motion, but the precise content of the legislative and policy changes was mainly determined by domestic factors.

Going back to the problem of 'double standards' and, especially, the lack of an internal minority policy, the following comment can be made in regard to the alleged problem of lack of EU competence concerning minority protection. An analogy with human rights seems in order. The EU does not have an explicit competence in relation to human rights. Nevertheless, the European Court of Justice (ECJ) has identified a duty to respect human rights for the institutions and the member states when they are operating in the field of EU law. It can be argued that, in order to respect human

rights, some kind of regulation/legislation on fundamental rights is needed in relation to the existing explicit competencies of the EU. This mainstreaming of human rights in the EU has ultimately resulted in the adoption of the EU Charter on Fundamental Rights.

It is generally accepted that minority rights are part and parcel of human rights. Hence the duty to respect human rights entails an obligation to respect minority rights, as has been confirmed by the European Commission and as is explicitly confirmed in Article I, 2 of the draft Constitutional Treaty. In other words, there would already be, under current EU law, a duty on all member states to respect minority rights (when operating in the field of EU law).

Some experts have pointed to the following existing EU competences where this minority protection mainstreaming could be very meaningful. Article 151(4) of the EC Treaty (1957) has been qualified as a basis for mainstreaming regional cultural diversity, which could indirectly benefit territorially concentrated cultural and linguistic minorities. Similarly, Article 13 of the EC Treaty, and the expanded prohibition of discrimination in EC law, have a great deal of potential, since it is now no longer limited to gender and EU nationality but also encompasses religion, and racial and ethnic origin as prohibited grounds of discrimination. The Racial Equality Directive (2000/43/EC), which has been adopted on the basis of Article 13, is generally considered to have (at the moment) most potential for internal minority protection. This Directive not only tackles differentiation on the basis of racial or ethnic origin, but can also – through the concept of indirect discrimination – address certain differentiations on the basis of language or religion. As pointed out above, this prohibition of indirect discrimination *if interpreted progressively* can be understood as imposing on the member states a duty to reasonably accommodate differences, also differences in identities and lifestyles. It is to be hoped that this potential development will actually take place.

The Directive has a very broad material and personal scope of application. The material scope is not limited to the employment sphere but also targets education, health care and social security. The degree to which the dimension of political participation is covered will have to be clarified by the jurisprudence of the ECJ. Finally, the Directive also sets out to address the traditional problems of actual enforcement of the prohibition of discrimination.

It should be underlined that third-country nationals (immigrants or 'new' minorities) can benefit from this Directive. While Article 3(2) excludes differentiations on the basis of nationality as such, it has been justly claimed that when a differentiation on the basis of nationality could be qualified as indirect racial discrimination, it would be covered nevertheless. Clarification of case law of the ECJ on this (and other aspects) of the Racial Equality Directive is eagerly awaited, but so far no cases are pending.

While it is still true that there is no coherent internal minority policy in the EU, there does seem to be an emerging awareness that the EU cannot remain indifferent towards the faith of minorities. While the overarching value of cultural diversity seems a likely avenue for minority-friendly internal measures, references in the founding treaties to cultural diversity arguably focus on diversity between states rather than diversity within states. However, there are a few exceptions, like Article 151(4) and the duty to respect cultural diversity expressed in Article 22 of the Charter of Fundamental Rights. Article 22 has been construed as a 'minority' provision by the EU Network of Independent Experts on Fundamental Rights, but this body has no legislative or judicial power.

Be that as it may, there are increasing references to 'ethnic minorities' (often side by side with 'immigrants') in the social inclusion programme. While this is focused on the employment sector, it is interesting that the 2006 report on social exclusion of the European Commission and the Council of Ministers states that 'the exclusion of people and groups, such as immigrants and ethnic minorities, from participation in work *and society* [should be addressed] for economic as well as social justice reasons'. Furthermore, one of the key priorities is to 'improve access to quality services and to overcome discrimination and increase integration of … ethnic minorities and immigrants' (8–10). Admittedly, little attention is paid to identity issues, but, as was already pointed out, it is *possible* that identity themes will also be addressed (in terms of the prohibition of indirect racial discrimination). The main focus, however, is on employment, as was also visible in the name of the Advisory Group

established by the Commission in January 2006, namely the 'high-level advisory group on social integration of ethnic minorities and their full *participation in the labour market*'. Hopefully, this attention to minorities and their fate in official policies and documents will translate into a more positive reality for these groups.

In view of the ongoing resistance of certain states in relation to minorities (e.g. Belgium, France and Greece), it is unlikely that the founding treaties will ever contain an explicit competence in relation to minorities. This was also noticeable in the elaboration of the Draft Constitutional Treaty. The protection of minorities is marked as a foundation value of the EU. Although this was a big step forward for minorities, there are still no explicit competences assigned to the EU to make this more concrete.

It remains to be seen how the 'mainstreaming' of attention for minorities will develop, and whether the ECJ, in its jurisprudence on human rights as a general principle of EC law, will take up the position of the Commission that minority rights are a component part of human rights, and hence that the actions of states in the field of EC law have to comply with minority rights. If anything, it will be a very incremental process.

Minority issues in the European states: recurring problems

The regional report on Europe (pp. 89–102) provides an excellent overview of the recurring problems in relation to minority protection in the European states. Hence it suffices here to highlight those themes that are particularly problematic in terms of participation (in the broad sense).

The systemic discrimination against the Roma is not confined to Eastern European states but can also be witnessed in Western European states. Similar problems of exclusion from economic, social and political life have also been remarked in relation to the North African communities (new minorities) in several states. Nevertheless, it should be acknowledged that in the wake of the (duty to) grant EU citizens electoral rights in local elections, Denmark, the Netherlands and Sweden also grant electoral rights to non-EU nationals after 3–5 years of residence. So far this does not seem to have had a significant impact on the overall level of economic (or social) participation of the population groups concerned. More seems to be needed to counter prejudice against immigrant groups.

The practice of several countries of introducing advisory bodies for immigrants or minorities is to be welcomed as an important mechanism for representation and participation. However, there is scope for such bodies to be better institutionalized.

Since 11 September 2001, anti-Muslim sentiment has been gaining ground in several, if not most, European states. Governments should pay special attention to the danger that the application of anti-terrorist measures does not disproportionately target Muslims. This unjustifiable disparate impact would amount to a violation of the prohibition of indirect discrimination.

Finally, it should be underlined that unreasonable linguistic requirements in relation to access to jobs, to nationality or to the passive right to vote, similarly could amount to indirect racial discrimination. While the problems of the Russophone minority in Estonia and Latvia in this respect are well known, other governments should also take care to avoid such requirements, in view of the resulting serious impairments of various dimensions of participation.

Trends, prospects and suggestions

The above overview has revealed a complex patchwork of outright positive developments, developments with potential to improve minority protection but also negative developments that need to be addressed urgently.

At the level of the states themselves, the question of political will is very important, not least because the minority rights standards themselves leave states a considerable amount of discretion. Political will on the part of states matters not only at the level of implementation but also at the level of the adoption of (new) standards. In this respect, the call to adopt an additional directive to tackle the particular integration problems of Roma can be highlighted.

The discretion left to states concerning implementation also underscores the importance of adequate monitoring systems. It is striking that the lack of judicial supervision of the FCNM has not prevented the contracting parties from taking up the suggestions of the AC by way of an incremental process. The jurisprudence of the ECHR reveals that there is a great deal of potential but that the Court so far has not made full use of

it, often because of the margin of appreciation it allows states.

It remains to be seen to what extent the process of internalization of minority protection in the EU will proceed. In this respect, the case law of the ECJ, inter alia in relation to the Racial Equality Directive, and the possible place of minority rights within human rights as general principle of EC law, is eagerly awaited. ▪

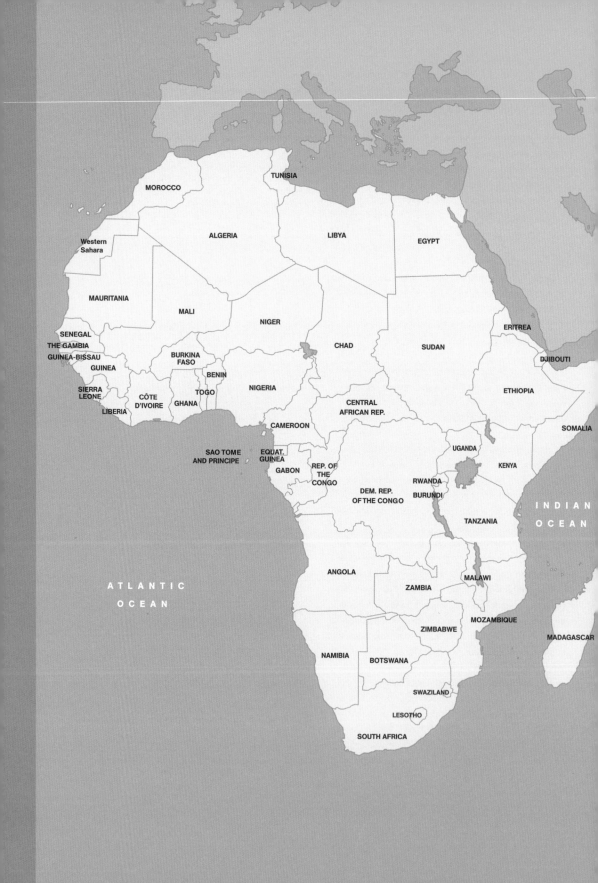

Africa

Eric Witte

On the whole, conditions for minorities in Africa remained bleak during 2006, and were clearly worse in those places where minorities lacked representation. Mass atrocities in Darfur intensified following a May peace agreement that largely excluded two important minority groups. Likewise, a July 2006 peace agreement in the Cabinda region of Angola appeared to be in jeopardy following the exclusion of key Cabindan factions. In Nigeria, conflict in the Niger Delta region continued unabated as credible representatives of Delta minorities were largely excluded from discussions about the sharing of oil revenues and that issue's link to endemic violence. In other parts of Nigeria, systematic exclusion of minorities in the name of 'indigeneity' fuelled ethnic violence. In the Horn of Africa, pastoralist minorities competing for ever scarcer resources came into worsening conflict with each other, even as they remained under-represented in government institutions dealing with their plight. At the end of 2006, the US-backed Ethiopian military action to break the grip of the Islamist alliance in Somalia raised the spectre of a growing conflict, drawing in many different foreign actors, as the humanitarian plight of Somalis worsens.

Liberia saw improved prospects as new President Ellen Johnson Sirleaf aimed to include all ethnic groups in her government and emphasized the empowerment of girls and women. Burundi had reason to hope that cyclical inter-ethnic atrocities might finally cease as the final rebel faction signed up to a peace agreement. Though still suffering from years of brutal conflict, the Democratic Republic of the Congo went to the polls for the first time in 40 years with the hope that an elected government might finally end the rampage of warlords who have brought suffering to all of its many minorities and chronic sexual violence to Congolese women.

West Africa
Côte d'Ivoire
A stand-off continues between a government dominated by southern ethnic groups, notably those of the Akan linguistic-cultural area and the minority Bété (of which President Laurent Gbagbo is one), and northern New Forces rebels largely consisting of Muslim ethnic Dioulas (Mandé) and Senoufos. For decades, Côte d'Ivoire had one of Africa's strongest economies and attracted large immigrant

communities from Burkina Faso and Mali, many of whom stayed for generations, but whose citizenship is now disputed by many southerners.

The seeds of the current conflict were sowed in 1999 when Robert Guei (himself a Yacouba, a minority group along the Liberian border) seized power in a 1999 military coup and promoted his predecessor's xenophobic notion of 'Ivoirité' to question the citizenship of northerners, and to sideline prominent northern presidential candidate Alassane Outtara in 2000. Laurent Gbagbo replaced Guei following troubled elections that same year, but embraced 'Ivoirité', and his supporters killed scores of northerners. Northern army units mutinied in September 2002 and the resulting clashes killed thousands, leaving the country *de facto* partitioned.

Apart from a spike of violence in November 2004, an international buffer of 7,000 United Nations (UN) peacekeepers and 4,000 French troops has been successful in preventing the resumption of large-scale clashes. Following the failure of peace agreements in January 2003 and July 2004, the two sides signed a new compact in April 2005. The agreement aimed to address northern concerns about identification, nationality and electoral laws; it led to the demobilization of militant groups linked to President Gbagbo and provided for a transitional power-sharing government until elections in October 2005. With lagging implementation and tension still palpable, the UN Security Council approved an extension of the provisional government until October 2006, albeit under an internationally appointed prime minister alongside President Gbagbo.

In November 2006, with elections cancelled and leaders on both sides of the north–south divide cultivating ethnic division, the UN Security Council extended this arrangement until October 2007 elections. Though the Security Council resolution transfers military and civilian authority from President Gbagbo to appointed Prime Minister Charles Konan Banny, Gbagbo immediately announced that 'any articles, any clauses in the resolution which constitute violations of Côte d'Ivoire's constitution will not be applied'.

Liberia
In January 2006, Ellen Johnson Sirleaf was inaugurated as Liberia's new president. She pledged

to end the political manipulation of ethnicity, empower Liberia's women, and pursue broad economic development. In February, Johnson Sirleaf inaugurated a Truth and Reconciliation Commission tasked with helping the country face the past and overcome its divisions. At her request, the following month Nigeria surrendered former President Charles Taylor to Liberia for delivery to the international war crimes tribunal in Sierra Leone. In a stunning break with warlordism and impunity in Africa, he now awaits trial in The Hague, while Liberia seeks to overcome the deep scars to which he contributed.

Around 95 per cent of Liberia's population consists of 16 indigenous ethnic groups, with Americo-Liberian descendants of freed slaves making up most of the rest. Americo-Liberian elites established Liberia in 1847, employing divide-and-rule practices and limited voting rights against indigenous Liberians to maintain dominance until 1980, when Samuel K. Doe overthrew the ruling party. Rather than empowering all indigenous Liberians, Doe built a brutal dictatorship based on favouritism for his small ethnic Krahn and related groups. His persecution of such other minorities as the Gio, Grebo and Mano fuelled a December 1989 insurgency led by Charles Taylor.

Rallied to 'kill the Krahn', Taylor's forces engaged in years of brutal conflict against other factions and West African peacekeepers before Taylor assumed the presidency in 1997. His repression of disfavoured minorities encouraged a new rebellion in 1999. As rebels advanced on the capital – and following announcement of his indictment for war crimes in neighbouring Sierra Leone – Taylor fled to Nigeria in August 2003. After two years of transitional government noted for weak leadership and corruption, in November 2005 Ellen Johnson Sirleaf won the presidency with broad support from diverse ethnic groups.

Nigeria

In the course of 2006, Nigeria, the most populous country in Africa, strained under its complicated federal system, the political manipulation of ethnicity, and unrest over resource sharing.

The Igbo (Ibo), Hausa-Fulani and Yoruba peoples make up around 65 per cent of Nigeria's population, but there are over 250 ethnic groups. During the colonial era, Britain gave preferred educational opportunities to the largely Christian populations of the south, with northern Muslims relying to a great extent on Koranic education. Beginning in colonial times, there have been varying attempts to manage or exploit Nigeria's ethnic, religious and linguistic diversity through various forms of federalism. Since 1996, the country has been divided into 36 states and 774 Local Government Areas.

Beginning with the country's 1979 Constitution, the concept of 'indigeneity' has been perpetuated in the current 1999 Constitution. This system categorizes all Nigerians as indigenes or non-indigenes (also labelled 'settlers') to a region based on where their parents or grandparents were born. The mechanism's intent was to ensure ethnic parity in education and employment, as well as to protect traditional cultures. But in 2006 Human Rights Watch and the International Crisis Group separately reported that the principle has instead systematically marginalized millions of Nigerians and encouraged ethno-linguistic identity politics that have fanned the flames of inter-communal violence, even where the roots of many conflicts lie elsewhere or pre-date policies of indigeneity. The mere definition of which groups are indigenous to a region creates many controversies; disputed historical migration patterns and intermarriage often make clear delineations impossible. The policy has become a tool for indigenes across the country to exclude competing 'settlers' from scarce educational and employment opportunities, even if these are life-long residents of the community. Not surprisingly, this has led to fierce resentment among the excluded.

For example, in diverse Plateau State, indigeneity has been used by Christian politicians to maintain dominance through exclusion of Muslim Hausa and Fulani 'settlers'. The Jarawa ethnic group is also classified as 'non-indigene', although it also fails to qualify for indigenous status anywhere in Nigeria. Between 1999 and 2004 in Plateau State, inter-communal fighting arising from disputes over indigeneity, land and religion resulted in 250,000 internally displaced persons. April 2006 fighting between members of the Pan and Gomai ethnic groups over issues of indigeneity resulted in over 100 killed and 8,000 displaced persons.

In the wake of the September 2005 publication of Danish cartoons depicting the Prophet Mohammed, in February 2006 Muslim mobs attacked minority

Christians in northern Nigeria, killing 16 and burning 11 churches. The government deployed soldiers and riot police to contain the violence.

Niger Delta

Oil from the Niger Delta has made Nigeria the world's twelfth largest oil producer and accounts for 95 per cent of its foreign currency revenue. Despite high world oil prices, such minority groups of the Niger Delta as the Ijaw and Ogoni remain mired in poverty, lacking in education and jobs, and suffering from oil companies' pollution of their air and water. Nigeria's 1999 Constitution gives the central government ownership of the country's natural resources. Most of the derivative percentage passed back to state and local accounts is stolen by corrupt officials. Tensions have mounted, with ethnic resistance groups in the Delta increasingly turning to violent means. Militants launched a series of attacks on oil installations in January and February 2006. In April, President Olusegun Obasanjo proposed a 'Marshall Plan' for the Delta, but only with involvement of corrupt local officials and exclusion of many civil society organizations that enjoy credibility in the region. Following further attacks, in August 2006 Obasanjo ordered a crackdown on militants while still pursuing negotiations. The abduction of oil workers in October 2006 pointed to continuing radicalization among minority populations of the Delta, and an ongoing need to address the causes of their anger.

North Africa

Algeria

In 2006 the Berber minority of Algeria, comprising 20–30 per cent of the population, viewed with trepidation a possible thaw in the relationship between the government and Islamic militant organizations, all the more so following attacks on Berber political leaders.

In 2001, years of agitation for greater recognition of their Tamazight language, music and culture culminated in rioting. Implementation of vague January 2005 government concessions to Berber demands stemming from the unrest has been overshadowed by a *rapprochement* between the government and Islamic extremists. In February 2006, the cabinet of President Abdelaziz Bouteflika declared a six-month amnesty for government forces and most Islamist militants who were involved in

the civil war of the 1990s if they agreed to disarm, but by its expiration fewer than 300 militants had accepted the offer. The sweeping 'law implementing the charter on peace and national reconciliation' also criminalized discussion of the conflict. Some Berber organizations that favour a secular Algerian state, such as the Movement for Autonomy in Kabylie, feared that the Bouteflika government was getting too close to the Islamists, even as this relationship remained ambivalent. In October 2006, the president of the Popular Assembly in the Tizi Ouzou province of the Kabylie region was shot and killed. The government blamed Islamic militants for this and two other assassinations of Berber leaders over the previous 13 months.

Egypt

Continuing religious intolerance in Egypt during 2006 led Christian Copts to seek the protection from the government, and the Baha'i minority to fear that government's active role in their torment.

The Copts are Egyptian Christians, mostly Orthodox, who trace their roots to Pharaonic peoples and their conversion to the arrival of St Mark in the first century AD. Nationally, Copts make up around 5–10 per cent of the population but are more concentrated in Cairo and Alexandria and comprise an estimated 18–19 per cent of the population in southern Egypt. They face state discrimination in such areas as university admissions, public spending, military promotions and required authorizations for the building or repair of churches. Islamist attacks on Copts have led the latter to fear legalization of Egypt's largest opposition force, the Muslim Brotherhood. April 2006 knife attacks on Copts outside churches in Alexandria led to sectarian violence.

Whereas *Shari'a* law recognizes Coptic Christians as 'people of the book', no such tolerance exists for the tiny Baha'i community of 500–2,000. Baha'i is a religion with roots in Shia Islam that emanated from Persia in the nineteenth century. Because the Baha'i believe that God's word is passed to humans through an ongoing series of revelations, it clashes with Islam's view that the Prophet Mohammed's revelations were the final ones. Currently, many Baha'i believers in Egypt are denied birth certificates and the identification required to open bank accounts or enrol their children in school, and their marriages are not recognized. The Egyptian government is appealing a court ruling from April 2006 that allows Baha'i to have identity cards listing their faith. A related government report in October 2006 argued that Baha'is must be 'identified, confronted and singled out so that they can be watched carefully, isolated and monitored in order to protect the rest of the population as well as Islam from their danger, influence and their teachings'.

Morocco: Western Sahara

In 2006, Morocco continued in its refusal to allow a referendum in Western Sahara that might end the long-standing impasse with the Saharawis in that occupied land.

The Saharawis of Western Sahara are traditionally nomadic herders, now largely urbanized, of mixed Berber, Arab and black African descent. They speak a dialect of Arabic called Hassaniya. In 1975, the colonial ruler Spain ceded Western Sahara, which is rich in phosphates, fisheries and suspected offshore oil, to Morocco and Mauritania. That same year the International Court of Justice (ICJ) found that neither had legitimate claims to territorial sovereignty over the region. The Saharawi opposition, the Polisario Front, fought both countries. Mauritania withdrew in 1979, ceding its claim to Morocco, against whom the rebels fought for 16 years with Algeria's support. Of a population of around 250,000, some 160,000 Saharawis fled to refugee camps in southern Algeria, where they remain today. The conflict ended with the introduction of UN peacekeepers in 1991, and the expectation that there would be a referendum on self-determination in accordance with the 1975 ICJ ruling and subsequent UN resolutions.

Morocco has consistently refused to allow a referendum and, in October 2006, the UN Security Council extended the 15-year-old UN peacekeeping mission for a further six months. Following a May 2005 crackdown by Moroccan authorities, a September 2006 UN report leaked to the press raised concerns about Saharawis suffering police brutality, torture, lack of freedom of expression or due process. Nevertheless, Moroccan ally France blocked proposals to include these concerns in the latest UN resolution prolonging the peacekeeping force. A controversial July 2005 fishing agreement between the EU and Morocco, pending approval by the European Parliament, would allow EU fishing vessels to catch in occupied Western Sahara's rich coastal waters.

Central Africa
Angola: Cabinda

Hopes of progress to end the conflict over the oil-rich enclave of Cabinda faded in that latter half of 2006 as the government sidelined a civil society organization representing the minority population.

The Bakongo people of Central Africa make up around 14 per cent of Angola's population, and the preponderance of the 300,000 people of the northern Angolan province of Cabinda. Cabinda is separated from the rest of Angola by the sliver of the Democratic Republic of Congo that runs to the Atlantic. Though tiny in size and relative population, the area represents an estimated 60 per cent of Angola's vast oil reserves.

The natural resource has raised the stakes for Cabindan efforts to achieve self-determination that date back to 1961. With the end of Angola's civil war in 2002, fighting in Cabinda between separatists and the Angolan army intensified, resulting in widespread human rights abuses against Cabindans. From March 2006, an umbrella organization, the Cabinda Forum for Dialogue (FDC), entered into discussions with the government. In July 2006, the government banned one element of the FDC: Cabinda's only human rights organization, Mpalabanda. In August one Cabindan rebel leader signed a separate peace with the government that was disavowed by other Cabindan factions. The head of Mpalabanda was arrested in September 2006 and released one month later, pending trial for 'instigating, inciting and condoning crimes against the security of the state'. Chevron, the largest oil operator in Cabinda, conceals the amount they pay to the Angolan government. Non-governmental organizations (NGOs) criticize the oil giant for contributing to graft that only fuels resentment among the impoverished Cabindan population.

Burundi

In 2006, war-torn Burundi had reason to hope that it could finally end decades of mutual atrocities between its Hutu majority and Tutsi minority as the last rebel group signed up to a peace agreement and transitional justice mechanisms were being developed to help the country process its tortured history.

The population of Burundi is 85 per cent Hutu, 14 per cent Tutsi and 1 per cent Twa. Although Tutsi pastoralists generally enjoyed privilege in pre-colonial

Right: Election materials stockpiled in the warehouse of the Independent Electoral Commission. The Democratic Republic of Congo's first multi-party elections in over 40 years were held in July 2006. Sven Torfinn/Panos Pictures

times, colonialism and political manipulation following the country's independence in 1962 sharpened ethnic differences, and these eclipsed other social divides. Successive Tutsi military regimes oversaw several massacres of Hutu, notably in 1972, when between 100,000 and 200,000 Hutu were killed and 300,000 forced to flee the country. The assassination of a newly elected Hutu president in 1993 sparked an uprising that resulted in 100,000 Tutsi deaths; the Tutsi-dominated army killed tens of thousands of Hutu in retribution. Fighting continued throughout the decade, exacerbated by the 1994 genocide in neighbouring Rwanda. Throughout, the small Twa minority of forest dwellers suffered at the hands of both Hutu and Tutsi fighters.

The 2000 Arusha Accords created a transitional government. By 2003, one of two hold-out Hutu militias had signed up to the peace agreement, and UN peacekeepers arrived in 2004. In 2005, Burundians voted overwhelmingly to approve a new power-sharing constitution with ethnic quotas for representation in government, administration and the military. In August 2005 elections, Pierre Nkurunziza and his Hutu-dominated party, a former rebel faction that allegedly committed massive human rights abuses, took control of every branch of government. The election campaign saw intra-Hutu rivalries overshadow the Hutu–Tutsi divide. In April 2006, the government deemed the situation in Burundi safe enough to lift a midnight-to-dawn curfew that had been in place since 1993. Amid halting progress on political reform, tempered by continued reports of government torture and other human rights abuses, the last hold-out Hutu militia signed a peace agreement in September 2006. Despite a limited amnesty granted to these rebels, the government and UN are moving forward with creation of a special war crimes court and a Truth and Reconciliation Commission.

Democratic Republic of the Congo

In 2006 the first democratic elections in nearly 40 years offered some hope that the Democratic Republic of the Congo (DRC) might finally

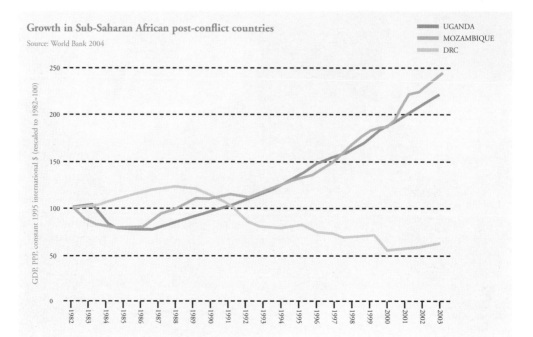

Growth in Sub-Saharan African post-conflict countries

Source: World Bank 2004

UGANDA
MOZAMBIQUE
DRC

GDP, PPP, constant 1995 international $ (rescaled to 1982=100)

250
200
150
100
50
0

1982 1983 1984 1985 1986 1987 1988 1989 1990 1991 1992 1993 1994 1995 1996 1997 1998 1999 2000 2001 2002 2003

overcome ethnic divisions long exploited by domestic and foreign powers for political and material gain. Against the backdrop of deep ethno-linguistic divides, a devastated economy and the militarization of much of the country, the democratic election of incumbent President Joseph Kabila and his party's strong showing in elections to the weak national Parliament may have signalled a new chance for the DRC, but by no means assured its peaceful future.

The DRC is a geographically diverse country the size of Western Europe, with a population of almost 60 million made up of hundreds of ethno-linguistic groups. Throughout its history of brutal exploitation as a personal fiefdom of Belgian King Leopold II from 1881 until 1908, Belgian colonial rule until independence in 1960, and its plundering by US-backed dictator Mobutu Sese Seko during the Cold War years, the territory's ethnic diversity has been manipulated to serve the interests of those seeking to control its tremendous wealth of natural resources, including rubber, timber, gold, copper, cobalt, coltan and diamonds.

Following the 1994 genocide in neighbouring Rwanda, many Hutu extremist perpetrators joined hundreds of thousands of Hutu refugees who feared retribution in eastern DRC (then still known as Zaire). From there, the militants, with the support of

Mobutu, launched attacks on the new Rwandan government as well as on Congolese Tutsi, the Banyamulenge. In 1996 Rwanda and Uganda sent their own forces into Zaire, and backed the rebel Laurent Kabila in a westward sweep through the vast country. In the process, Rwandan government forces and Kabila's forces killed thousands of Hutus, combatants and non-combatants alike. Mobutu fled as Kabila took the capital Kinshasa in May 1997 and renamed the country DRC. However, Kabila quickly fell out with Rwanda and Uganda, and in 1998 these countries sponsored rebel movements to invade the DRC anew. The rebels also had the support of Burundi, while the Kabila government had that of Angola, Namibia and Zimbabwe. Seven nations were now involved and, because their various roles were often rewarded with natural resource concessions, they had little incentive to withdraw. Fighting continued despite a July 1999 ceasefire agreement and deployment of an understaffed UN peacekeeping mission (MONUC) in 2000. A study by the International Rescue Committee found that between 1998 and 2004 nearly 4 million people in the DRC – the equivalent of the entire population of Ireland – died as a result of the war.

Laurent Kabila was assassinated in January 2001 and his son, Joseph Kabila, assumed the presidency. Under international pressure, he entered into a power-sharing government with rebel factions and civil society in July 2003. Violence in the north-eastern Ituri province flared, despite the improved situation in Kinshasa, and French-led European Union (EU) peacekeepers intervened in 2003 to quell the violence in and around Ituri's capital Bunia. In July 2003 and October 2004 the UN Security Council bolstered MONUC to a nearly 17,000-strong force, and gave it a new mandate to protect civilians 'under imminent threat of violence'. In April 2006, the EU approved deployment of additional peacekeepers to provide security for UN-administered national and local elections foreseen by the 2002 peace agreement that led to the power-sharing government.

Over 30 presidential candidates emerged during 2006 in a campaign marred by incitement to ethnic hatred. According to Human Rights Watch, in May 2006 one of DRC's four vice-presidents engaged in anti-Tutsi rhetoric at a campaign rally for Joseph Kabila in the North Kivu town of Goma. Another vice-president, and Kabila's main rival for the presidency, Jean-Pierre Bemba, was a leading Ugandan-backed warlord in north-eastern Congo prior to entering the government in 2003. He stands indicted in the Central African Republic in connection with a rebellion there, and is widely believed to be under investigation by the International Criminal Court. He based much of his campaign on xenophobic rhetoric aimed at casting doubt on Kabila's Congolese identity. When results were announced on 20 August 2006, Kabila had 45 per cent to Bemba's 20 per cent, requiring a run-off. The announcement sparked three days of violence between their supporters in Kinshasa that killed at least 23 people and required intervention by UN and EU peacekeepers.

The run-off election was held on 29 October and, despite violence in part of Ituri province, international observers deemed the voting to be largely free and fair. Kabila won with 58 per cent of the vote, mostly from the Swahili-speaking east, creating concern about his ability to overcome the divide with the Lingala-speaking west. Bemba lost his challenge of the results in court and, despite earlier violent outbursts by his supporters in Kinshasa, Bemba announced in late November that he would respect the election results.

The years of war since the 1996 and 1998 invasions have resulted in a proliferation of militias

and a spread of lawlessness, particularly in the eastern DRC provinces of Ituri, North and South Kivu, and Katanga. The Kinshasa government and invading forces alike have established ethnically based militias, including local Mai-Mai defence forces, usually organized along tribal lines. Armed factions were encouraged by their sponsors to prey on local populations for subsistence and looted goods. The larger context of DRC's chaos and natural resource wealth combined with marauding, predatory militias has sharpened various ethnic conflicts, put the country's minority groups at risk and resulted in staggering levels of sexual violence against women.

Inter-communal violence has gone well beyond that associated with the divide between Hutu and Tutsi/Banyamulenge, most prevalent in North and South Kivu. Tensions between Hema and Lendu peoples, incited during colonial times and the Mobutu era, have destabilized Ituri province. As the power-sharing government was taking shape in 2002–3, clashes between heavily armed Hema and Lendu militias and massacres of civilians resulted in at least 50,000 deaths and sparked EU intervention. Despite a demobilization programme, extended in July 2006, there were reports in September 2006 that splintered Hema and Lendu militias were re-arming and engaging in new clashes. In Katanga province, allies of Kabila engaged in violent intimidation of the opposition, consisting largely of the Luba people who have roots in Kasai province.

As MRG found in 2002, even Twa or Bambuti (pygmy) peoples living deep in the forests of eastern DRC had become targets of various militias, including that of Jean-Pierre Bemba. Militias target the Twa in order to deprive rivals of Twa hunting skills and knowledge of forest paths. Twa women have been singled out for rape due to the belief that sleeping with them confers special powers on the rapist.

All of DRC's many minority groups, and especially women, remain under threat from an unprofessional government army and the many militias. Their greatest hope rests with efforts to overcome the country's corruption, mal-governance, impunity and lack of state control in the east.

Rwanda

During 2006, the Tutsi-dominated Rwandan Patriotic Front (RPF) government continued to pursue policies of playing down ethnicity as a means of overcoming the minority's endangerment – all too evident in the 1994 genocide that claimed an estimated 800,000 Tutsi and moderate Hutu victims at the hands of Hutu nationalists. Rwanda's population consists of 85 per cent Hutu, 14 per cent Tutsi, and 1 per cent Twa.

Critics claim that its bans on 'divisive' parties and organizations are designed to serve RPF power interests. In February 2006, Rwanda's first post-genocide president, Pasteur Bizimungu – a Hutu – lost an appeal against his 2004 conviction for 'criminal association' in his attempt to form a rival party in 2002. Human Rights Watch documented flaws in his first-instance trial.

In the course 2006, the International Criminal Tribunal for Rwanda (ICTR) continued to hear top-tier genocide cases, while Rwanda's traditional *gacaca* courts continued to try large numbers of less prominent cases. In January 2007, the Rwandan cabinet voted to abolish the death penalty. If approved by parliament, the move will allow countries which object to the death penalty to extradite genocide suspects back to Rwanda. Abolition of the death penalty was also a pre-requisite for the transfer of some ICTR cases to Rwanda's national court system. The ICTR prosecutor still hadn't taken up serious allegations of war crimes committed by the RPF's predecessor, the Rwandan Patriotic Army, during the genocide. The prosecutor faced the implicit threat that if he did so the government would rescind all cooperation with the tribunal.

The indigenous Twa people of Rwanda, numbering an estimated 25,000–30,000, remain on society's margins, disadvantaged in education, health care and land rights. The government of Rwanda has threatened to cut off all assistance to the Twa and their organizations if they continue to consider themselves as a distinct people.

Uganda
Acholi
In Uganda during 2006, the search for an end to the brutalizing war of the north gathered pace, as the Lord's Resistance Army (LRA), notorious for abducting children and turning them into killers, signalled a willingness to negotiate following its leaders' indictment in 2005 by the International Criminal Court (ICC) for war crimes and crimes against humanity.

Under British colonial rule the Acholi people of northern Uganda were favoured for service in the police and army. When Milton Obote seized power in 1966, four years after independence, he surrounded himself with Acholi and other northerners, and repressed southern peoples. Idi Amin, himself a northerner from the minority Kakwa group in the West Nile area, unleashed horrific retribution against the Acholi from 1972 to 1979. Rebel leader Yoweri Museveni, a southerner, came to power in 1985, and brought increasing stability and prosperity to Uganda, with exception of the north.

For 20 years, the Acholi have been victimized by the LRA. The rebel group receives support from the Sudanese government and are led by an erratic Acholi named Joseph Kony. The LRA has abducted an estimated 25,000 children over the years, forcing them to commit heinous atrocities against the Acholi people. In response, Museveni's government has forced 1.4 to 1.9 million civilians into camps where they remain prone to attack by the LRA and the national army alike, and unable to grow their own food. The ICC issued arrest warrants for Kony and four other LRA leaders on charges of war crimes and crimes against humanity in February 2005. Through 2006, the LRA has insisted on immunity from prosecution in exchange for an end to the fighting. Acholi opinion on the matter is divided. Negotiations are continuing despite the international indictments; the discussions included a meeting between Kony and UN Under-Secretary-General Jan Egeland.

Batwa
In July 2006, the Uganda Land Alliance for Coalition of Pastoral Civil Society Organizations warned that the few thousand Batwa (Twa) of Uganda are in danger of extinction. The organization's report warned of starvation and loss of social cohesion among desperate Batwa who lost their homes in the Bwindi Impenetrable Game Park when this became a World Heritage Site for preservation of endangered mountain gorillas in 1992.

East Africa
Ethiopia
The efforts of Prime Minister Meles Zenawi to control separatism in Ethiopia appeared to be unravelling in 2006, as various ethnic movements drew inspiration from government repression and

lack of democratic participation.

Ethnic liberation movements toppled former Communist dictator Mengistu Haile Mariam in 1991, and Meles Zenawi, the leader of the Tigrean People's Liberation Front, set about organizing the state as an ethnic federation, albeit one in which he would lead co-opted representatives of other ethnicities under a single-party umbrella: the Ethiopian Peoples Revolutionary Democratic Front. This proved a particularly difficult undertaking as Tigreans comprise only around 6 per cent of the Ethiopian population. Prime Minister Meles's re-election in flawed May 2005 balloting only deepened the resentment of other ethnic groups.

This was especially true of Ethiopia's Amhara people, about 30 per cent of the population of the country. The Amhara are prominent in the political opposition and suffered in the government crackdown on protests at election fraud, which resulted in at least 193 deaths and 763 injuries.

In February 2006, the government arrested thousands of Oromo – an ethnic group making up approximately 30–50 per cent of the country's population – following its protests of the election irregularities called for by the rebel Oromo Liberation Front (OLF) in the south of the country. In September, two senior Ethiopian military officers defected to the OLF.

In December 2006, the Ethiopian military, backed by the USA, took on the Islamist alliance in neighbouring Somalia, driving it from control of the capital Mogadishu on 28 December. Ethiopia is the principal backer of the weak Somali transitional federal government headed by President Abdullahi Yusuf Ahmed. Prime Minister Meles Zenawi justified the invasion by citing national defence interests, claiming that the Islamists had been infiltrated by al-Qaeda. Sabre-rattling by the Union of Islamic Courts – calling for a holy war on Addis Ababa, and overt support for the Ogaden self-determination groups – raised tensions in 2006. Two wars have already been fought over the Ogaden region in the South-East of the Ethiopia, where the majority of the population is ethnic Somali. Although Ethiopia has vowed to withdraw its forces completely from Somalia, it is unclear whether the promised AU peacekeeping mission will transpire. Without Ethiopian military support, a question-mark remains over the TFG's ability to hold onto the territory seized in December's offensive.

Meles also faced rebellions among smaller ethnic minority groups. The Anuak – traditional hunters, farmers and fishers – make up approximately 1 per cent of the country's population, and for centuries have lived in the area that is today's Gambella region of south-western Ethiopia. The Anuak have lived alongside, and in competition with, Nuer pastoralists. Under the Mengistu regime, the Anuak faced considerable suppression as the authorities seized land and forcibly conscripted Anuak villagers for service in the army and on collective farms. Some 60,000 peasants, mostly lighter-skinned 'highlanders' from other parts of Ethiopia, were also forcibly resettled in Gambella. Tensions have risen as competition for land and water has intensified.

In recent years, the Meles government has also moved against the Anuak, with human rights activists reporting murder, rape and torture. The government has increased the military presence in the area following attacks by militants. It argues that the military action is targeted at the rebels – but Anuak leaders claim that civilians are also being targeted. In April 2006, there were reports that the Ethiopian army was cooperating with the Sudan People's Liberation Army to disarm Anuak along the border. Amnesty International reported in May 2006 that, in the previous two and a half years, the Ethiopian government had detained 900 Anuak opposition members without trial, though it had released 15 former senior officials in December 2005. Tensions rose again in June 2006 when attackers thought by aid workers to be Anuak militia members ambushed a bus travelling from Addis Ababa to Gambella, killing an estimated 14–30 civilians. In the immediate aftermath, water and power were cut to Gambella town, and Ethiopian troops and highlander militias enforced a curfew. In September 2006 a Dutch humanitarian NGO reported that more than 44,600 internally displaced persons – Anuak, Nuer and Highlander alike – were living in camps and in dire need of assistance.

Oil is another factor in this dispute. Although in May 2006 the Malaysian oil company Petronas announced that its first test well in the area had proved barren, land use rights in Gambella remain contentious, and efforts to discover oil could yet intensify the struggle for control of the region.

Horn of Africa: Pastoralist peoples

Across the Horn of Africa, traditionally nomadic herders are suffering from competition for land worsened by drought and regional conflict. In turn, their dire situation is increasingly driving them into conflict with each other, as well as non-pastoralist peoples.

Traditionally pastoral peoples of Kenya, including Borana, Gabra, Maasai, Pokot, Samburu, Somalis and Turkana, have long seen the land available for their herds diminish. Under British colonialism, whites carved out large estates in fertile areas that had earlier been used as communal grazing lands. At independence in 1963 much of this land made its way into the hands of Kenyan elites. The establishment of national parks and game reserves also pushed nomadic herders out of their traditional lands. For example, the Endorois community has been evicted from the Lake

Bogoria area in the Rift Valley, and the Monchongoi forest on the Laikipia Plains, to make way for a game reserve and ruby mining. The community has not received adequate compensation for their eviction, nor has it benefited from the tourism in the reserve.

In recent years, the area of pasture lands available to pastoralists has been further reduced through a failure of multiple rainy seasons widely attributed to global warming. As pastures and water have become scarcer, pastoralist peoples of Kenya and neighbouring states have come into conflict over what little remains.

A March 2006 cattle raid launched by the Pokot people of north-western Kenya into Uganda sparked a response from the Ugandan army, and at least four civilians were killed. A UN official in Uganda observed that, 'the first aim is normally not to steal animals, but to monopolize the water source'. By May, in response to the killing of at least 19 people in cattle raids over the course of the year, the Kenyan government had launched an operation aimed at collecting up to 30,000 illegally held weapons in

western Kenya. Local Pokot and Samburu people claimed that the operation was undertaken without adequate consultation and had sparked the flight of thousands of pastoralists across the border.

Pokot cattle raids continued in 2006, driving thousands of Samburu into camps, and have been marked by widespread murder and rape. In October, Samburu pastoralists pressed claims to ancestral rights to graze their cattle on private farms in Laikipia and government forces moved in to forcibly evict the herders. Similarly, Maasai herdsmen drove cattle into the Masai Mara game reserve to protest what they claimed was a corrupt allocation of 4,000 acres of park land to an elite Maasai developer.

In October, MRG and the Centre for Minority Rights Development brought together women from various pastoral communities in Kenya to discuss common problems. The participants underscored the lack of women's representation within their communities, and the lack of adequate representation of pastoral peoples in the Kenyan government.

In south-western Tanzania, in May 2006, the government began the eviction of hundreds of pastoralists from riverbeds in Mbeya in order to prevent further environmental degradation caused by their cattle. Likewise, following poor March–May rains across the region, competition for land in southern Ethiopia has led to conflict. In June, Oxfam reported that clashes between Guji and Borena peoples over pasture land had resulted in at least 100 killings and the displacement of thousands.

MRG is supporting an initiative to establish a regional council of traditional pastoralist elders from Ethiopia, Kenya, Tanzania and Uganda. It is hoped that, as water and available pasture land become scarcer, elders can work together to resolve conflicts and determine equitable sharing of what resources there are.

Somalia
According to MRG's People under Threat calculation (Table 1, Reference section, pp. 118–23), Somalia is the most dangerous place in the world for minorities. Throughout 2006, tensions between Ethiopia – the main backer of the weak transitional federal government (TFG) – and an alliance of Islamist parties escalated. The US-backed Ethiopian military offensive broke the grip of the Islamist alliance, but ushered in the prospect of further instability and conflict, in a country

which has been without a central government since 1991. Ominously, foreign actors – in the Middle East, and the Horn of Africa region, as well as the US – have become increasingly involved in this round of the fighting. However, the roots of the conflict are to be found in inter-clan rivalries. According to the International Crisis Group, the Union of Islamic Courts became a platform for powerful Hawiye clan, after many sections of this influential grouping felt excluded from the TFG. The TFG's head President Yusuf is from the large Darod clan – as are many in the higher ranks of the TFG. After December's crisis, the president faces faces calls from the international community to form a more inclusive government. As the fighting spread, many Somalis fled. Pastoralist peoples already suffering hardship from the twin disasters of drought and heavy flooding in 2006 – have been especially vulnerable. By October 2006, UN officials estimated that 1000 refugees a day were arriving in North-Western Kenya. In early 2007, the Kenyan government shut its border with Somalia, drawing strong criticism from the United Nations Refugee Agency (UNHCR). Humanitarian agencies continue to warn that lack of access to refugees is exacerbating an already dire situation.

Sudan: Darfur
Despite a peace deal hailed in May 2006 and a subsequent UN Security Council resolution that called for the deployment of a robust peacekeeping force, the latter part of the year saw an intensification of fighting, mass killings and displacements in the Darfur region of Sudan. The year 2006 also witnessed the continued unwillingness of the international community to intervene on behalf of targeted black civilians, whom many observers regard as victims of an active genocide.

In Arabic, Darfur means 'home of the Fur', who are black Nilo Saharan sedentary farmers. The western region is also home to other black tribes, notably the Masalit and the Zaghawa, who are semi-nomadic pastoralists, as well as various Arab camel- and cattle-herding peoples. Worsening drought over the past 25 years created tension between pastoralists and agriculturalists in competition for land and was intentionally exacerbated by the Sudanese government. Its divide-and-rule tactics injected mounting frictions with racism, and spurred nomadic Arabs to band together to form Janjaweed militias that targeted black Africans. In response, beginning in the 1980s, the Fur, Masalit, Zaghawa, and other, smaller ethnic groups began forming their own militias. Whereas the North–South war in Sudan that lasted from 1983 to 2005 pitted Arab Muslims in the North against black Christians and animists in the South, all groups involved in the Darfur conflict are predominantly Muslim.

In early 2003, Fur, Masalit and Zaghawa militias engaged in skirmishes with government forces. Following initial setbacks for the Sudanese army, then still preoccupied with fighting in southern Sudan, the government turned to the Janjaweed. Heavily armed by Khartoum and backed by the Sudanese air force, the Janjaweed launched devastating assaults against the opposing militias over the course of 2003 and 2004. It also targeted Fur, Masalit and Zaghawa villages, killing thousands and displacing tens of thousands within Darfur and across the Sudanese border to Chad. In February 2004, the International Association of Genocide Scholars labelled the atrocities in Darfur 'genocide', followed unanimously in July 2004 by the United States Congress.

Although the UN and many governments sought to avoid this term – and the associated obligation to intervene in accordance with the 1948 Genocide Convention – those who did adopt the finding, including US President Bush in September 2004, proved equally unwilling to take effective action. Instead, the international community vested its hopes in a small, under-funded and under-equipped African Union (AU) peacekeeping force that first deployed in August 2004. By September 2005, the AU force had increased to 7,000 soldiers but, despite its best efforts, was still ill-trained, ill-equipped and incapable of protecting Darfuri civilians under attack in an area the size of France.

A January 2005 peace agreement between Khartoum and south Sudanese rebels envisioned power-sharing and broad autonomy for the South, but excluded Sudan's other disgruntled regions, including Darfur. As the death toll in Darfur rose into the hundreds of thousands, and atrocities such as the systematic rape of black Darfuri women by Janjaweed forces became well established, the International Criminal Court announced in June 2005 that it was launching an investigation into alleged violations of international humanitarian law.

The international community touted as a major breakthrough an AU-brokered peace agreement for Darfur signed in Abuja, Nigeria, in May 2006. Yet only one of the three main Darfuri rebel factions – that most closely aligned with the Zaghawa people – signed the agreement with Khartoum. Absent the agreement of the other two main factions, for the most part closely aligned with Fur and Masalit tribes, violence intensified in the weeks following the agreement.

With increased violence came new calls for the UN to take over peacekeeping responsibilities in Darfur, notably by AU heads of state meeting in July 2006. Sudan's leader, Omar Bashir, rejected the idea out of hand, and that same month the Sudanese air force resumed attacks on Darfuri villages for the first time since the May peace agreement.

At the end of July, UN Secretary-General Kofi Annan proposed deployment of a UN force of 24,000 and, on 31 August, the Security Council approved a smaller but robust force of 17,000. However, at the insistence of China and Russia – tied to Khartoum through oil development and weapons trafficking – deployment of the force hinged on Sudan's invitation. By November 2006, President Bashir had repeatedly made it clear that no such invitation would be forthcoming. Instead the AU agreed to extend its force through the end of the year.

In October a former Janjaweed fighter confirmed to the BBC that the militias were under direct control of the Khartoum government, which had directly ordered the killing and raping of civilians. He alleged that Sudanese Interior Minister Abdul Rahim Muhammad Hussein frequently conveyed such instructions personally to Janjaweed fighters.

Minority Rights Group International (MRG) released a report in October 2006, which found that the catastrophe in Darfur could have been prevented if early warning signals had been recognized and acted on. The report said that instead the UN and its member states had repeated in Darfur many of the same failings as in their response to the 1994 Rwandan genocide. In particular, policy-makers had failed to take account of Khartoum's long-standing efforts to foment ethnic division in the region.

Southern Africa
Zimbabwe and South Africa
Zimbabwe's economy continued its implosion during 2006, and the Ndebele people, prominent among the opposition Movement for Democratic Change (MDC) and distrusted by the government of

President Robert Mugabe, continued to bear the brunt of his regime. The Ndebele make up around 16 per cent of the country's population. Shortly after his 1980 election, following the ouster of white supremacist Ian Smith's regime, Mugabe summoned nationalism among the Shona people – comprising about 70 per cent of the population – to consolidate his power and sideline his greatest liberation rival, the Ndebele tribesman Joshua Nkomo. It is estimated that Mugabe's 'Gukurahundi' pogrom in the Ndebele heartlands of Matabeleland and the Midlands from 1983 to 1987 resulted in 10,000–20,000 killings. In recent years, Mugabe has discriminated against opposition supporters, and thus many Ndebele, in distribution of food aid necessitated by his economic policies. In October 2006, Mugabe's party spokesman resurrected bitterness over Gukurahundi, saying he had no regrets about the atrocities.

In 2006, it was estimated that 85 per cent of Zimbabweans lived in poverty and in 2007 the country's inflation rate has reached 1,600 per cent. An estimated 3–5 million impoverished Zimbabweans have fled the former breadbasket of southern Africa to South Africa, where they have become targets of resentment and face the prospect of grim migrant holding camps.

South African whites have expressed nervousness that Jacob Zuma, a leading candidate to succeed current President Thabo Mbeki, has not sufficiently distanced himself from Mugabe's policies of land redistribution, which, beginning in 2000, stripped some 4,000 white Zimbabweans of their farms and precipitated Zimbabwe's economic meltdown. Many among South Africa's black majority are impatient with the pace of economic improvement after Apartheid, and the continued white ownership of most fertile land. They clamour for land redistribution, although in Zimbabwe most confiscated land ended up in the hands of elites or unskilled and largely unsuccessful subsistence farmers, all regime supporters

Botswana

In December 2006, the Basarwa – also known as the Khoesan or San – in Botswana won a historic legal victory when the country's High Court ruled that the Basarwa had been illegally forced out of their ancestral home in the Central Kalahari game reserve. The panel of three judges ruled 2–1 in favour of the Basarwa. Judge Mpaphi Phumaphi

said the treatment of the remaining Basarwa in the game reserve amounted to 'death by starvation', as they were prohibited from hunting, or receiving food rations. Judge Unity Dow ruled that the government had 'failed to take account of the knowledge and culture' of the Basarwa when it expelled them. However, the verdict also said the government was not obliged to provide basic services to anyone wishing to return to the reserve, nor had it acted illegally by terminating essential services in the game reserve.

The Basarwa are believed to have lived in area covered by the Central Kalahari game reserve for 20,000 years, but their hunter-gatherer lifestyle and unique traditions have come under intense pressure in modern Botswana. The government claims that the Basarwa have voluntarily moved from the Kalahari into resettlement camps, where the authorities are better able to provide education and health services. But campaigners maintain they have been forcibly resettled. Before the court case, hunting in the game reserve was prohibited and Basarwa caught breaking the law were arrested. But the High Court ruled that it was illegal to refuse to issue the Basarwa with special game licences. It also found that the refusal to allow the Basarwa into the Central Kalahari game reserve was unlawful and unconstitutional. There are persistent allegations of harassment and ill-treatment of the Basarwa at the hands of the police and wildlife officers. Critics also say the resettlement camps have exposed the Basarwa to HIV/Aids – Botswana has one of the highest rates of infection in the world.

Concerns about the Basarwa's treatment were also highlighted by the UN Committee tasked with monitoring the implementation of the International Convention on the Elimination of Racial Discrimination, which Botswana ratified in 1974. In its 2006 response to a country report submitted by Botswana, the Committee recommended that the government resume negotiations with the residents of the reserve with a view to finding a 'solution acceptable to all'. The Committee also noted the difficulties experienced by poor people – many of whom belonged to the Basarwa – accessing law courts, because of high court fees, and the problems facing children who did not belong to the majority Tswana tribe, because education was not sufficiently tailored to minority linguistic and cultural needs. ■

Alaska (US)

CANADA

NORTH
PACIFIC

UNITED STATES

ATLANTI
OCEAN

Hawaiian Islands (US)

MEXICO

CUBA

DOMINICAN REP.

HAITI
Puerto Rico (US)

BELIZE   JAMAICA

GUATEMALA   HONDURAS
EL SALVADOR   NICARAGUA

COSTA RICA
PANAMA

VENEZUELA

GUYANA

COLOMBIA

SURINAM
Guyane (Fr.)

ECUADOR

PERU

BRAZIL

BOLIVIA

PARAGUAY

SOUTH
PACIFIC

CHILE

URUGUAY

ARGENTINA

Americas

Maurice Bryn

The Americas display a diverse indigenous and minority profile. Besides large populations of mixed ethnicity, there are significant numbers of people of African descent as well as immigrants from European, Asian–Pacific, Arab and other Middle Eastern countries.

The most disadvantaged and vulnerable minorities continue to be those of African and indigenous origin. Even when examining specific national trends, such as the substantial growth of Latino/Hispanic minorities in the USA to almost 42.7 million, in the end this involves largely indigenous, African descendant or Afro-indigenous and *mestizo* migrant populations from Central and South America and the Caribbean.

Americas: Afro-descendants

African descended populations represent a majority on most of the islands of the Caribbean and constituted substantial minorities in many Central and South American states; especially in Brazil, Colombia and Venezuela, as well as the USA.

The African presence in the Americas goes back to the earliest formation of colonial societies and is mainly – though not exclusively – the result of several centuries of large-scale importation of millions of people from the African continent to provide forced labour on plantations and in mines and other commercial enterprises.

Although forced labour was instituted mostly for economic reasons, racist beliefs became entrenched. Across the Americas mainstream society continues to favour white people and assimilationist cultural values. As a result, the main issues affecting the Afro-descendant minority population group today are still mostly related to discrimination and exclusion.

In Caribbean and Latin American economies, discrimination against Afro-descendant citizens is effected in the public and private sector through preferential hiring and credit practices, racial profiling by law enforcement agencies and insufficient allocation of government resources in the public sector.

This has a particularly negative impact on both African descended and indigenous people, who share a history of discrimination, marginalization and exclusion that continues to affect their present socio-economic condition.

Nevertheless, in countries such as Brazil, Canada, Cuba, the USA and Venezuela, Afro-descendant individuals have increasingly attained high-level positions in the government, military and private sector. However, as a group this population continues to experience significant covert and overt discrimination and racial prejudice, and they still make up the poorest strata of their national societies.

Human rights organizations in the Americas reported in 2005/6 that most Afro-descendant populations continue to have severe disadvantages in education, income, health, life expectancy, literacy and employment.

Countries with statistics disaggregated by race, such as Brazil, Canada, Colombia and the USA, continue to show a persistent socio-economic gap between blacks and whites. According to *The State of Black America 2005*, the income level of African-American families is only one-tenth that of white families, 78 per cent of Afro-Brazilians live below the poverty line, compared to 40 per cent of white Brazilians. According to the World Bank, Afro-Colombians, although they constitute approximately 25 per cent of the entire population, represent well over 75 per cent of the poor.

In the Caribbean area, decades of studies have also suggested that Afro-Puerto Ricans are disproportionately present in deprived urban neighbourhoods and low-paid informal-sector employment. This is hardly different from Cuba, where Afro-Cubans live in the most neglected parts of cities such as Havana. Moreover, Afro-Cuban activists continued to report, in 2006, that most Afro-Cubans remain economically marginalized from the dollarized tourist sector and external investment initiatives, and have to create their own informal sector opportunities.

Most of the predominantly Afro-descendant areas in the Americas continue to be poorly served or completely lacking in many basic services and social programmes. The majority of the region's Afro-descendant population continued to live in isolated rural communities or overcrowded urban zones, with poor health, education and social services. Many of these locales lack adequate roads, electricity, communications and water supply, and appear to have been abandoned by federal, state and municipal governments.

This discrimination is especially evident in legal responses, and in the allocation of national resources and social sector investment. Mainstream political and economic elites continue to ignore the acute economic and social problems that affect the region's Afro-descendant populations and the zones they inhabit. In great measure this is essentially a reflection of their *de facto* invisibility as a population group.

Statistical invisibility

Despite a long historical – and substantial contemporary – presence in the Americas, Afro-descendant minorities continue to be subjected to official and statistical invisibility. Even though numbering in the tens of millions in some countries, Afro-descendants are still not recognized or acknowledged as a distinct cultural group in the national constitutions of states such as Bolivia, Brazil, Mexico, Peru or Venezuela. The presence of small historical Afro-descendant populations in Argentina, Chile and Paraguay is also still officially ignored. Recently, in a break from the national norm, the state of Oaxaca became the only government entity in Mexico to officially recognize Afro-Mexicans as a distinct ethnic group.

Afro-descendant activists continue to argue that the first step towards addressing invisibility and related socio-economic disparities is the collection of disaggregated census data on African descended populations in these and other countries.

In Venezuela in 2005, the Network of Afro-Venezuelan Organizations pressured the Chávez government to collect data on Afro-Venezuelans in the next census. Similar advocacy is also taking place in Bolivia, Costa Rica, Ecuador, Honduras and Peru. Through the *Todos Contamos* programme supported by the World Bank and Inter-American Development Bank, Colombia received funds to incorporate racial indicators into the recent 2005 census. Similarly, Bolivian government authorities in the state of Santa Cruz agreed to a census of Afro-Bolivians for 2006.

Moreover, Afro-descendant activists continue to highlight the need for census methodologies that adequately capture how African descendants describe themselves. Only 1 per cent of blacks self-identified as 'Afro-Colombian' in that country's official census; however an independently conducted survey conducted by the City of Cali in 1998–9, based instead on self-descriptions by skin colour, found that over 30 per cent of residents at that time identified themselves as black or mulatto. This resulted in a radically different Afro-descendant count from the official version.

Political participation

There is a notable increase in Afro-descendant participation in the political processes of a number of countries in the Americas. Following the 2002 election, for the first time in its history, Brazil appointed four Afro-Brazilian national ministers, three of whom were women. This pattern of inclusion is set to continue with the re-election of President Lula da Silva to a second term in October 2006. Likewise, in Suriname, Afro-descendant Maroon political parties participated in the May 2005 national elections, with voters electing eight Maroon representatives of whom three obtained cabinet positions.

Afro-Ecuadorians have gained more visibility through the presence of black politicians and Afro-Ecuadorian non-governmental organizations (NGOs). In Peru, there were three Afro-Peruvians in the 2004 Congress. However, while the election of Evo Morales in Bolivia in 2005 promised to end Afro-Bolivian exclusion, in mid 2006 there were complaints about the lack of Afro-Bolivian candidates included in the new Constituent Assembly.

In 2006, there was one Afro-Uruguayan representative in Congress, who made efforts to increase general awareness of the country's African ancestry and cultural heritage and to promote positive discrimination in congressional policy.

Significantly, in the USA just as in Latin America, the African-American minority remains massively politically under-represented. Despite constituting 12 per cent of the US population, African-Americans currently hold only about 2 per cent of political offices across the country, and, at the highest level, even fewer – notwithstanding the appointments of Colin Powell and Condoleezza Rice during the Bush presidency.

This is hardly any different from Panama where, despite their high numbers, Afro-Panamanians remain markedly absent from positions of political and economic power. As of 2004 there was one Afro-Panamanian in the 13-member National Cabinet and the Solicitor General was an Afro-Panamanian woman.

In spite of their small numbers, since 1996 Afro-Costa Ricans have increasingly become elected representatives and gained cabinet-level appointments. This includes the 2005 nomination by the Citizen Action Party of a female Afro-Costa

Left: Indigenous Bolivian man in Cochabamba holds a sketch book showing his vision of Bolovia's new Constituent Assembly

Rican for the vice-presidency of the nation. Similarly, in Canada in 2005, Her Excellency the Right Honourable Michaëlle Jean of refugee Haitian origin, who migrated to Canada in 1968, became the first Afro-descendant woman to be sworn in as Governor General of Canada.

In the USA, the disenfranchisement of large numbers of the Afro-descendant minority continues to be of concern. Denial of voting rights particularly affects minority communities, whose residents make up a disproportionate number of those held in the US prison system. An estimated 2 million African-American and Latinos have lost their right to vote because of felony convictions and incarceration.

There are now 39 states in the US legislatively supporting the reinstatement of the voting rights of former offenders. In June 2005, both Iowa and Rhode Island took legislative steps to restore voting rights to parolees and probationers.

Profiling and incarceration

This problem points to an ongoing issue of unequal legal treatment and the remarkably high rates of incarceration experienced by Afro-descendant populations in most of the countries of the Americas; especially in Brazil, Colombia, Cuba, Dominican Republic, Panama, Puerto Rico, the USA and Venezuela.

This is largely a reflection of the strong racial prejudice that operates against African descendants. Discrimination is particularly violent in poorer areas, where police forces often act with impunity and racial profiling is rampant. In the USA, principally, there were continuing concerns in 2006 about the extraordinarily high incarceration rates and long sentence periods for African-American and Latino minorities. These are far higher and longer than those for white Americans. Consequently African-Americans, who only constitute 12.9 per cent of the US population, make up 38.9 per cent of that country's prison inmates.

Likewise, in Brazil investigators found that Afro-Brazilians receive longer sentences than white counterparts for the same crime and are more likely to suffer discrimination in prison. This matched the USA, where, despite an ongoing debate, convictions

for crack-cocaine possession (mostly non-white users) continue to be harsher than for powder-cocaine (mostly white users), leading to the disproportionate imprisonment of black, Latino and Native Americans.

There is increasing concern in the USA that the legal system is now affecting an even higher percentage of non-white women than men. In its March 2005 report, Fair Laws for Families revealed that, since 1986, there has been an 800 per cent increase in the number of African-American women behind bars in state and federal prisons.

Rights activists also point out that, because of the discriminatory patterns of arrest and excessive use of physical and deadly force against African-descendants, they are much more likely than other group to end up dead after encounters with the law enforcement agencies.

With the USA being one of the few Western democracies still employing the death penalty, blacks are sentenced to death four times more often than whites. A December 2005 study by the University of Maryland indicated that those who killed a white victim were still two to three times more likely to be sentenced to death than those who killed a non-white.

A report by the UN Special Rapporteur on Torture also found that most torture victims in Brazilian prisons were of Afro-Brazilian descent. The Institute of Applied Economic Research (IPEA) found that Brazil's people of colour are five times more likely to be killed by police than whites, and the Institute for Religious Studies (ISER) found that, in the extra-judicial police killings that were investigated, 64 per cent of the victims were shot in the back at close range and the majority were of African descent.

Also, in Cuba, activists continued to report that approximately 80–90 per cent of that country's large prison population are estimated to be Afro-Cubans, who only make up about 50 per cent of the national population. The same pertains in nearby Puerto Rico, where sociological studies indicate that Afro-Puerto Ricans still disproportionately occupy youth detention centres.

Racial prejudice is particularly rampant in the identification of potential offenders based on looks – also known as 'racial profiling', In February 2005, Afro-Canadian police officers in Toronto testified that racial profiling was an existing policy and that

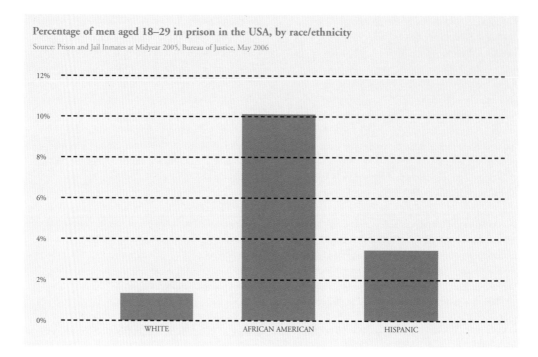

Percentage of men aged 18–29 in prison in the USA, by race/ethnicity

Source: Prison and Jail Inmates at Midyear 2005, Bureau of Justice, May 2006

12%

10%

8%

6%

4%

2%

0%

WHITE   AFRICAN AMERICAN   HISPANIC

they themselves experienced racism on the job. The same pattern is again revealed in Cuba where, although there are many Afro-Cuban police officers and army-enlisted personnel, racial discrimination in policing is common. In 2006, Afro-Cubans continued to complain of frequent and disproportionate stops for identity checks.

In Puerto Rico, many people from the Dominican Republic are classified as black and 'mulatto'. However, there is also a significant native Afro-Puerto Rican population, consequently local authorities sometimes arrest Afro-Puerto Ricans, assuming them to be illegal Dominican migrants. Likewise, police in the Dominican Republic often arrest Afro-Dominicans, assuming them to be illegal Haitians. Once in the USA, police similarly target both Puerto Ricans and Dominican immigrants.

Racial profiling by the police, immigration and airport officials is particularly widespread in the USA. The recent concern about terrorism has only exacerbated the problem. Following the attacks of 11 September 2001, profiling has greatly expanded. Approximately 32 million Americans have reported being victims of racial profiling. In Canada, the targeting of young African-Canadians, including those from Somali and Rastafarian communities, continued to be a major concern in 2006. The

African Canadian Legal Clinic attributes this increase to the new Canadian Anti-Terrorism Act (ATA). Moreover, Somali Canadians, being Muslim, are doubly discriminated against.

Besides Canada, Rastafari in the Caribbean also continue to be a vulnerable minority. Reports persisted of Rastafari being profiled because of hair length and beards, and being subjected to harassment and discrimination by both the state and private sectors.

Conflict

In Colombia, after years of isolation, the zones inhabited by Afro-Colombians have now become the most affected by the ongoing war. Almost four years after the most violent massacre in the history of Colombia's 40-year conflict in 2002, when 119 people were killed in a small Afro-Colombian fishing village, the Association of Afro-Colombian Municipalities reported in 2005 that as many as 40 per cent of paramilitary and guerrilla recruits in coastal regions are now African descendants.

In 2006, ethnic tensions between minority groups such as African descendants and those of East Indian origin in Guyana and Trinidad continued to be driven by competition for political dominance. Following elections in August 2006, grassroots Afro-

Guyanese increased calls for greater inclusion of their community by the predominantly Indo-Guyanese-based governing party.

Haitian migrants and refugees have continued to endure particular troubles that set them apart from other Afro-descendants in their destination countries, particularly in the Dominican Republic and the Bahamas. In March 2006, a mob seeking to avenge the murder of the mayor of the village of Las Matas de Farfan in the Dominican Republic caught two Haitians, doused with them with gasoline and set them ablaze.

Themes and initiatives
The annual regional Meetings of Legislators of African Descent (last held in Costa Rica in 2005) have continued to be of particular importance to Afro-descendant leaders. In these encounters, delegates from 19 countries gather to discuss ways of fostering democratic participation; to reaffirm their Afro-descendant identities; and reiterate national government commitments to combat prejudice and exclusion.

The Inter-American Convention against Discrimination
Another important emerging initiative is the Inter-American Convention against Discrimination, currently under consideration by the Organization of American States (OAS). This proposal attempts to provide people of colour throughout the Americas with a regional mechanism to redress rights violations specifically related to discrimination. Currently, cases of racial discrimination need to be tried as generic human rights violations, since no OAS statute exists that oversees discrimination cases.

Activists see the creation of the Inter-American Convention as a vital step towards providing African descendants and other minorities with a form of redress in countries where national courts have been reluctant to tackle racial inequities.

Brazil has taken a leadership role in this initiative and is also the sole supporter of the Special Rapporteur for African Descendants; however, the initiative has been strongly opposed by the US government. Also, in Brazil, the policy debate has continued during the Lula da Silva presidency regarding how best to address discrimination/exclusion of the African-descended population. This has included discussions on whether to emulate the US model of positive discrimination, quota systems and the criminalizing of discrimination. However, in 2006 a group of prominent opinion-makers, including several leading Brazilian academics, wrote a controversial letter to the Brazilian press condemning quotas, while in the US itself there were increasing attacks and legal challenges to the policy of 'quotas' and 'reverse discrimination'.

In July 2005, Canada signed the Council of Europe's first Additional Protocol to the Convention on Cybercrime, Concerning the Criminalization of Acts of a Racist and Xenophobic Nature as Well as Hate-motivated Threats and Insults Committed Through Computer Systems. This is significant given Canada's close communication/cultural links with the USA. According to an October 2005 FBI report, 67.9 per cent of the victims of the 9,528 hate crimes in the USA were of African descent.

Inter-American Court of Human Rights and Afro-descendants
In June 2005, the Inter-American Court of Human Rights (IACHR) found the government of Suriname guilty of human rights violations in the case of the 1986 massacre at the Afro-descendant N'Djuka village of Moiwana and the intentional destruction of their property by a National Army unit. The IACHR ordered the government to pay reparations to each survivor, investigate the crimes and conduct a public ceremony recognizing state responsibility and apologizing to the N'Djuka people.

Also, on 8 October 2005, the IACHR ruled against the government of the Dominican Republic in the case brought on behalf of two Dominican girls of Haitian ancestry who were refused birth certificates.

In December 2005, the foreign ministry indicated that, even though the verdict was considered unjust, they would abide by it. However, in essence the government has rejected the ruling and legal decisions in 2006 indicate that the courts are determined to continue using 'transit' classifications for Dominican-born Haitians.

Americas: indigenous peoples
Significant numbers of indigenous nations live in the Americas. In Latin America, indigenous people number around 52 million, about 11 per cent of the total population. There are also another 2 million indigenous people in Canada and the USA.

The present indigenous populations are the descendants of the millions who settled the entire hemisphere for several millennia before the start of the European colonial era. They developed thousands of nations, each with a distinct language, political tradition and social structure, and material cultures that ranged from nomadic hunter-gathering to monumental high-culture civilizations.

Canada has 612 different indigenous nations. Colombia has more than 80 indigenous peoples, living in a variety of ecological zones. Ecuador has 14 distinct indigenous ethnic groups. In Bolivia, Guatemala and Peru, indigenous populations constitute as much as 63 per cent of the national total. Mexico, with 62 groups numbering over 15 million people, has the largest number of indigenous people of any country in the region.

From the beginning of European settlement, indigenous communities in the Americas have been affected by successive attempts at extermination, enslavement, massacres and violent dispossession by those wishing to claim their lands and the terrestrial and subterranean wealth they provide.

From the outset, indigenous populations have faced two main survival choices: either total cultural assimilation or complete marginalization and exclusion from a mainstream society that is heavily oriented towards European socio-cultural values and life choices, and that negatively prejudges and discriminates against the culturally different.

In a pattern remarkably consistent with that established from the very beginning of fifteenth-century colonial contact, indigenous people today continued to face significant political and economic discrimination, particularly the invasion and loss of their ancestral lands in all of the countries of the Americas.

Despite constitutional reforms in most of Latin America during the 1980s and 1990s that recognized indigenous rights, and even with legal measures such as the International Labour Organization's Convention No. 169 on the Rights of Indigenous and Tribal Peoples (1989), indigenous populations continued to be threatened by the inroads of investors and private enterprises onto their territories. Ironically, this is often encouraged by the same state authorities that are signatories to the supposedly protective treaties.

NGOs in almost every country in the hemisphere continue to complain that the major threat facing

indigenous people is their ongoing relentless dispossession of land by national settlers and expanding investment by international commercial interests. The latter include tourism, real estate development and natural resource exploitation – particularly mining, oil exploration and logging ventures. These activities invariably threaten the cultural and economic vitality of indigenous communities, as well as the natural environments they inhabit.

Indigenous peoples continued to display much higher levels of poverty, disease, malnutrition and illiteracy than the rest of the national populations. As for Afro-descendants, with whom they have historically shared the negative effects of forced labour and dispossession, the ongoing prejudice and discrimination against indigenous people continues to be a major issue.

In many countries across the region, racial and ethnic discrimination is a daily occurrence, especially for those rurally based indigenous individuals who leave their communities and venture into large urban areas. Furthermore, organizations like Amnesty International (2004) have found that indigenous females experience disproportionate levels of economic and social marginalization, and experience double discrimination based on their identity as both female and indigenous people.

In recent years, indigenous NGOs and advocacy groups have become increasingly mobilized locally and internationally to address some of the issues affecting them. However, there continues to be a remarkable lack of political will on the part of governments to honour their international and constitutional obligations, and consequently indigenous peoples' lives continue to be negatively affected.

Sometimes this has encouraged growing partnerships between indigenous rights activists and environmental movements. It has also widened the debate regarding the place and function of indigenous people in their societies, and the need for continued cultural preservation. For example, in Peru, NGOs seeking convergence of indigenous activism and global environmentalism have become involved in the protest campaigns of Ashaninka communities against logging and oil exploration corporations.

On the other hand, modernizing trends, including the advent of new communications technologies and increased physical access to formerly isolated indigenous areas, are prompting new cycles of change. In places such as the gold-rich rainforests of Brazil and the Guianas, consumer goods acquisition is increasingly becoming a measure of status and devaluing indigenous traditional agriculture and other socio-cultural practices.

Many of the large South American Altiplano and other *campesino* indigenous populations in the region have been marketplace oriented since the colonial period, including through slave/indentured labour and land dispossession. However, many lowland communities have tended to be smaller, more isolated and less connected to the national/global economy. This has often made them much more vulnerable to contemporary natural resource exploitation.

In an increasingly globalized environment, continuing poverty and the desire for material goods means that indigenous youth in these zones are increasingly seeking ways to join the contemporary cash economy. Finding opportunities for income generation has therefore become a major concern. This is especially because the loss of traditional land usually hastens cultural disintegration and brings an end to traditional means of survival.

In communities across Central and South America, and especially in the rainforest zones, land dispossession has continued, prompting new waves of indigenous migration into hostile urban areas to seek often poorly paid wage labour and to face a landless future that promises generations of struggle to escape from the bottom of the urban socio-economic scale.

Economic development
After centuries of interaction, increasing numbers of indigenous people of varying social classes now live in the region's urban areas, from Canada to Argentina, and in some cases have achieved economic and social standing greater than mainstream non-indigenous middle-class residents.

This is especially true in the wealthy industrialized northern countries like the US where half of the Native American population lives in cities and towns, largely integrated with the general population. In Canada, only about a quarter of all indigenous people still live on their ancestral lands, and a well-organized network of 117 indigenous-controlled Native Friendship Centres exists to provide services in urban areas.

Moreover, many North American indigenous nations continue to move increasingly towards economic self-sufficiency, with sizeable revenues being accrued from casinos, resource extraction and other ventures.

Nevertheless, for the vast majority of indigenous people in the Americas, the communities and areas where they live continue to be chronically impoverished and lack adequate education, housing, electricity, health and other social services. In Latin America, most indigenous people in 2006 continued to eke out a marginal existence as the poorest of the poor, using various subsistence measures to survive in remote, hard-to-reach, poorly serviced interior areas of their countries. This has a negative impact on family and environmental health, education and infant mortality.

Moreover, all across the Americas the municipalities and regions with the highest numbers of indigenous peoples continue to be among the poorest, regardless of the size and wealth of the country.

In the USA, Native American reservation housing is still substandard, often without electricity, indoor plumbing or refrigeration, except on the wealthiest reserves. In Canada, a Community Well-Being Index, developed by the Department of Indian Affairs and Northern Development (2004), found that, of the bottom 100 Canadian communities in the country, 92 were indigenous communities. In Chile, the 600,000 indigenous Mapuche remain among the poorest, least educated and most malnourished sector of Chilean society.

In cases where indigenous people are supposed to be owners of their resources, the issues of land titling, resource rights and revenues are still major concerns. Unregulated non-participatory resource extraction means that the major share of revenue usually goes to the state and does not benefit the indigenous economies. Consequently, indigenous rights issues are still closely linked to the demand for greater autonomy and social sector investment.

Land/property rights
In some countries like Canada, Colombia, Guyana and Nicaragua, indigenous groups have title to significant land areas. In September 2006, the Ministry of Amerindian Affairs of Guyana in South America indicated that 13 per cent of that country's land (11,205 square miles) has now been deemed to be indigenous property; however, this does not

include subsurface mining rights, which, as in the rest of Latin America, are still held by the government.

That is in contrast to the USA and Canada, where territorial rights include subsoil resources. Nevertheless, disputes persist. In March 2006, following urgent requests from the Western Shoshone people whose land claims cover 80 per cent of the State of Nevada, the UN Committee for the Elimination of Racial Discrimination (Early Warning and Urgent Action Procedure) called on the USA to freeze any plans to privatize Western Shoshone ancestral lands for transfer to multinational mining and energy interests, and to desist from activities being carried out without consultation.

Although, on paper, Latin American governments have shown an increasing willingness to begin the

process of land titling, this still did not translate into increased security, autonomy or greater material benefits. Despite new legislation or constitutional amendments promising respect for indigenous territorial rights, private interests and states' economic agendas are still prioritized over the demands of local indigenous communities.

Consequently, indigenous people continued to face the centuries-old limits on their ability to participate in decisions affecting their lands, traditions and natural resources, causing some indigenous organizations to engage in protests that

have sometimes led to violent confrontations.

In May 2006, Quichuan organizations in Ecuador set up a series of protests and roadblocks that led to the retreat of a US oil company. In Colombia, the U'wa peoples continued their struggle against oil exploitation in their territories, despite winning legal victories against multinational oil companies before the Colombian courts. Indigenous leaders in Paraguay have stepped up protest campaigns against deforestation and the pollution of water sources. Furthermore, the presence of international corporations and tourism operators on indigenous ancestral lands in Venezuela caused protests over the deterioration of the environment and indigenous peoples' traditional ways of life.

Among other land/resource rights issues across the region that have raised the concern of activists are petroleum discoveries on Maya land in Belize; rubber, tin, gold mining and cattle ranching on Urueu-Wau-Wau lands in Brazil; petroleum extraction on Waroani land in Ecuador; ranching on Ayoreo land in Paraguay and also on Yabrana lands in Venezuela; and gold, oil and mineral exploitation in Guatemala and Honduras.

In Brazil, French Guiana, Guyana and Suriname, a relentless increase in rainforest exploration and gold mining activities is bringing with it a host of irreversible social and environmental changes. In 2006, indigenous community groups in these countries continued to complain about the allocation of mining and logging rights without adequate consultation, and are particularly concerned about continuing environmental degradation and social disruption, including mercury poisoning, community violence, prostitution, alcohol abuse, youth suicides and family disintegration.

The link between culture and ecology is often at the heart of indigenous group survival across the Americas, and is invariably linked to safeguarding the environment.

In Honduras, the Tawanka are struggling to have their inhabited zone in the Moskitia rainforest declared an eco-cultural biological reserve. In Nicaragua's Caribbean Coast region, indigenous populations are seeking to safeguard their communal lands in the second largest rainforest after the Amazon. This area continues to be invaded by Pacific region settlers, who deforest lands for cattle-raising in a zone already designated as a Biosphere Reserve

Moreover, conflict between indigenous peoples and the state over land use and titling has also occurred in some instances where the stated aim is environmental and cultural preservation.

This includes archaeological parks of so-called Mayan ruins in Guatemala and the establishment of national parks in Argentina, French Guiana and Honduras. Indigenous leaders often cite lack of consultation and limited participation in planning processes, which do not take into account spiritual perceptions and traditional land-use patterns.

It should be noted that much of the conflict over inadequate consultation is related to disregard for, or non-compliance with, ILO No. 169, which commits governments to prior consultation with indigenous groups over development projects that may affect them, and also mandates compensation.

While Argentina, Guatemala and Honduras have ratified ILO No. 169, France has not. Indigenous groups in French Guiana, which is an overseas *département* of France – have had to base their arguments on the international agreements of the 2003 World Parks Congress of Durban, which require the involvement of local populations in all stages of protected area design.

Prevention of conflict/genocide

The continued dispossession of indigenous populations and the resulting protests are invariably accompanied by violence against indigenous leaders and rights activists in many Central and South American countries. In Honduras and Mexico, as in the rest of the region, leaders who speak out for political change are singled out for persecution by powerful landowners who wield inordinate influence over local police, and the political and judicial systems.

In Bolivia, systematic attacks, killings and other violent acts are perpetrated against indigenous Guarani leaders in the lowland region around Santa Cruz, carried out by thugs recruited by large landowners.

The Arhuaco lands in the high coastal Sierra Nevada region of Colombia in 2006 have continued to be the battleground between growers of illicit crops and the Colombian government, and in Venezuela the most serious threat facing the Wayuú is still their location, close to the war-torn Colombian border.

A particularly unsettling development for indigenous activists is the opportunistic attempt by some governments to link international anti-terrorism efforts to the suppression of local indigenous search for rights. In Chile the government's 2004 counter-terrorism legislation has been used against indigenous Mapuche fighting for territorial rights. This led to the arrest and imprisonment of many Mapuche leaders. International protests and prisoner hunger strikes pressured the government to agree, in 2006, that the anti-terrorist law would not be applied to those involved in communal actions related to the recuperation of indigenous lands. However, many Mapuche activists still remain imprisoned under Chile's counter-terrorism law.

This development must be seen in light of the consistent failure by Latin American governments to prosecute those who have consistently terrorized and perpetrated violence on indigenous rights advocates. In Honduras, there is continuing concern regarding the apparent inability of the authorities to pursue justice related to past assassinations and the continuing threats and harassment directed at Garifuna, Lenca and Xicaque–Tolupan indigenous land rights activists. Also, in Guatemala the government's efforts to acknowledge and prosecute abuses have been marred by charges of judicial corruption evidenced by the light sentencing in cases of gross violations of human rights. Few of the people responsible for the genocide of nearly 200,000 indigenous people during the 1980s civil war have been brought to justice.

Education reform

In seeking avenues to safeguard their rights, indigenous groups continue to explore ways to increase educational levels. Access to education continued to be a problem for many of the region's indigenous children. In addition to scholarships being allocated to indigenous secondary school students in a number of countries, indigenous organizations continued the debate over the form and content of bilingual/intercultural education programmes, many of which were mandated in the constitutional reforms of the 1980s and 1990s.

In what are often criticized as easy token gestures designed to conform to clauses of ILO No. 169, many governments – including El Salvador and Panama – have willingly engaged in bilingual education programmes, even in cases where the constitution does not guarantee it, such as Peru.

Ironically, in Peru, despite the much-publicized development of a Microsoft Word Quechua language program, many Quechua and Aymara reject bilingual education, arguing instead for better education in Spanish in order to properly confront the racism of mainstream Peruvian society and advance economically.

A similar debate exists in Guatemala, where, although a bilingual programme exists, children in densely indigenous municipalities are still taught in Spanish by indigenous teachers. By 2005 there were 7,832 schools in departments with significant indigenous Maya populations, but only 1,869 provided bilingual education. These concerns have practical origins and, in Guatemala, are partly connected to the restrictions of indigenous rights in judicial proceedings where, in 2006, many Maya continued to be tried in Spanish, even though they do not speak that language.

On the other hand, in Argentina the bilingual intercultural education issue has united members of Aymara, Chiriguano, Mapuche, Mbyá Guarani, Mocoví, Quechua, Toba and Wichi nations, and even non-indigenous linguistic minorities.

Still others in the Americas see cultural protection and bilingual education as important to social and ecological preservation. In most cases, however, curricula have failed to develop new methods or cultural knowledge content relevant to indigenous people's contemporary needs.

In Chile, Mapuche organizations continue to be involved in many schemes in rural and urban areas to try to reform the teaching methods as well as bilingual education content. This accords with other initiatives, such as eco-friendly tourism, which local Mapuche have often turned to their advantage, allowing them to publicize their 'cause' to foreign travellers.

However, in general across the region in 2006, bilingual education programmes continued to be constrained by a shortage of government resources and/or a lack of political will to enforce laws and implement local legislation or international treaty commitments. In many countries, efforts continue to be more theoretical than practical because of resource and training shortfalls.

Public participation

The issue of exclusion is particularly relevant in the political arena and progress has been slow. In most of the Americas, including those countries with large indigenous populations in the Yucatan and the South American Andes, political power continues to be in the hands of the *mestizo* elite. National political parties routinely restrict the election of indigenous members to the decision-making leadership posts within the internal party structures, thereby effectively excluding them from the wider political arena.

Changes are beginning to occur, however. Although not willing to self-identify as the first 'indigenous president' in the history of Bolivia, the election of Evo Morales in 2005 raised hopes for change across the region. The new government has implemented parliamentary reforms to encourage the increased participation of indigenous people at a national level. In July 2006 it was announced that an indigenous woman would preside over the new Constituent Assembly.

In Peru, where quotas now require that 15 per cent of candidates be indigenous, President Alejandro Toledo created the Instituto Nacional de Desarrollo de los Pueblos Andinos, Amazónicas y Afro-Peruano in 2004. This body, consisting of NGOs, sector ministry representatives and delegates elected by indigenous and Afro-Peruvian communities, promotes policy coordination between the government and indigenous organizations.

Chile is one of the few Latin American countries that has not provided constitutional recognition of indigenous people or ratified ILO Convention No.169. Congress has continually rejected the proposals and, overall in 2006, indigenous people continued to have barely any representation in the Chilean Congress and Senate.

Although Canada has never ratified ILO No. 169, nevertheless it has remained in the forefront of trends in the region towards reform and reconciliation between government and indigenous nations. This includes the granting of greater degrees of autonomy, self-government, land titling and indigenous control over resources. In January 2006, the incoming Conservative government in Canada indicated its commitment to continue this responsiveness.

Inter-American Court and indigenous rights

In 2006, the text of the Declaration on the Rights of Indigenous Populations in the Americas being developed by the Inter-American Commission on Human Rights (the Commission) still remains at draft stage, nevertheless indigenous groups have increasingly been taking their concerns to this international court.

In 1998, the Toledo Maya Cultural Council (TMCC) of Belize submitted a petition to the IACHR regarding government recognition of traditional Maya land rights and resource control, and calling for a moratorium on logging permits and other activities.

In late 2003, the IACHR issued a preliminary report on this case, built upon the jurisprudence of the precedent-setting *Awas Tingni* case (2001) against the government of Nicaragua, which for the first time ruled on the collective rights of indigenous peoples and mandated the government to title community lands.

According to the IACHR's ruling on Belize, the government violated the provisions of the American Declaration on the Rights and Duties of Man that affirm the rights to property and equality before the law by failing to protect Maya lands and resources, and by failing to obtain Maya consent for activities on their traditional lands, Despite the favourable IACHR decision, the Belize government in 2006 continued to issue leases, concessions and other interests that encumber Maya traditional lands.

The USA and most of the common law countries of the Caribbean have still not agreed to be bound by the jurisdiction of the IACHR; nevertheless, at the end of 2005, the Inuit Circumpolar Conference (ICC) submitted a communication to the IACHR claiming that the US failure to control emissions of greenhouse gases is damaging Inuit (Eskimo) livelihoods in the Arctic. ∎

Asia and Pacific

Joshua Castellino and Emma Eastwood

Pacific

A high proportion of indigenous peoples characterizes the populations of the Pacific states and, in 2006, differing trends for minorities were observed in the region. The Maori in New Zealand, who form a minority within their state, are seeing increased protection, yet ethnic Aborigines and Torres Strait Islanders in Australia remain vulnerable, with only a few notable land rights victories. The issue of new migrants is gradually assuming centre-stage in the region, with Asian migration to Australia and New Zealand and migration of Pacific Islander populations to other states in the region on the increase.

Australia

Australia is undergoing a troubled period in its relations with minorities and indigenous peoples. The government appears to be placing a stronger emphasis on 'Australian-ness', emphasizing a 'white' rather than a composite national identity. This reaction, against a backdrop of growing immigration of Asian/Muslim populations (currently close to 8 per cent of the population), is raising tensions in cities such as Sydney, as manifested in the violence on Cronulla Beach in December 2005. Following the same trend, Pauline Hanson, former leader of the One Nation Party, announced plans in December 2006 to make a come-back in the federal elections of 2007 on an anti-immigration platform; she has accused black African immigrants of bringing HIV/Aids to Australia.

Over the last two years, the replacement of the elected Aboriginal and Torres Strait Islander Commission by the government-appointed National Indigenous Council has denied Aboriginal nations (2.4 per cent of the population) effective political participation. Meanwhile, mining and other extractive industries see ever-increasing commercial values in Aboriginal homelands. The Aboriginal and Torres Strait Islander Act of 2005 (with amendments) that came into force in October 2006 needs to be monitored closely in this regard.

Despite the landmark 1992 *Mabo* decision concerning land rights, Australia seemed for a long time to be making little progress in terms of the recognition of native title. However, in October 2006, the Perth High Court ruled in favour of the Noongar people's claim, accepting a native title claim over urban land in the city. Political parties have expressed consternation over the result of the case, and the government has announced that it is preparing to file an appeal. In December 2006, an agreement was struck between the Githabul people and the New South Wales state government to share ownership of World Heritage-listed rainforests covering 6,000 sq km. The resolution of the land rights issue remains the key to reconciliation between Australian settlers and Australia's indigenous peoples.

Aboriginal life expectancy remains 20 years lower than that of other Australians, some Aboriginal languages are disappearing, and the nations face an

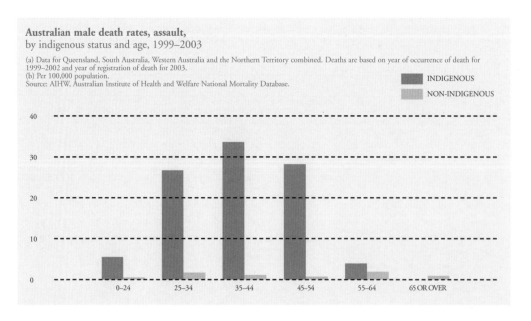

Australian male death rates, assault,
by indigenous status and age, 1999–2003

(a) Data for Queensland, South Australia, Western Australia and the Northern Territory combined. Deaths are based on year of occurrence of death for 1999–2002 and year of registration of death for 2003.
(b) Per 100,000 population.
Source: AIHW, Australian Institute of Health and Welfare National Mortality Database.

INDIGENOUS
NON-INDIGENOUS

array of other social problems. In December 2006, following a court ruling that there was not enough evidence to prosecute police involved in the death of an Aboriginal man in custody, indigenous leaders complained that 'Aboriginal lives can be taken with no consequences.'

Australia's 'Pacific solution' anti-refugee policy has seen it re-interpret its territorial dimensions to avoid responsibilities over intakes of refugees by establishing a 'clearing house' on the island state of Nauru to keep refugees away from the Australian mainland.

The Tasmanian government's apology in 2006 for its role in the Stolen Generations scheme (where Aboriginal children of mixed descent were taken from their families and settled with white families between approximately 1900 and 1969) goes against this trend. The apology, announced alongside a compensation package of AU $4 million (US $3.12 million), provides a model for other states, although thus far they have been reluctant to acknowledge their responsibility for the policies of eugenics that have been perpetrated against the Aboriginal nations for more than a century.

New Zealand

Although similar in many respects to Australia, New Zealand handles indigenous and minority rights issues in a different way. The Maori account for close to 15 per cent of the total population of the state, a further 6.5 per cent consists of Pacific Islanders,

while Asian immigrants account for another 8 per cent. The issues attendant on reconciliation between the white settlers and the Maori population are being examined by the Waitangi Tribunal, which was created by the New Zealand government in 1975. Like other Truth and Reconciliation processes, the findings of the Tribunal are not legally binding; however, they are respected by society and inform a basis for *rapprochement*. Progress before the Tribunal, although slow, has remained positive in 2006. While the fundamental issue of land return or compensation is at the forefront (with a Governmental Fiscal Envelope of NZ $1,000 million or US $687 million), most land claims remain outstanding, with Maori owning only 5 per cent of the country's land. Away from the land rights issues, Maori continue to face lower life expectancy and higher rates of unemployment, though the direction of the statistics would indicate the situation is improving.

Pacific Islanders have not benefited from government schemes aimed at the Maori and are disproportionately represented in unemployment statistics. They also form a higher proportion of the urban poor. The popularity of the racist New Zealand First party, at its zenith in 1996, appears to have waned (it won 5.72 per cent of support, garnering seven seats in Parliament in the 2005 elections). However, hostility has been reported towards Asian, and particularly Muslim immigrants, with vandalism

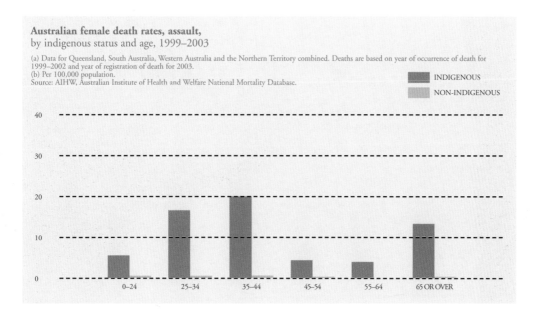

Australian female death rates, assault,
by indigenous status and age, 1999–2003

(a) Data for Queensland, South Australia, Western Australia and the Northern Territory combined. Deaths are based on year of occurrence of death for 1999–2002 and year of registration of death for 2003.
(b) Per 100,000 population.
Source: AIHW, Australian Institute of Health and Welfare National Mortality Database.

INDIGENOUS
NON-INDIGENOUS

Left: The Naxi, an ethnic minority numbering 280,000 people in China's Yunnan and Sichuan provinces, practise the ancient shamanistic religion of Dongba. This Dongba text is written in the last living hieroglyphic language in the world. Dermot Tatlow/Panos Pictures

of mosques in the aftermath of the 7 July 2005 bombings in London. In 2006, there were police calls for Muslim women wearing the *burqa* to be banned from driving – a move that sparked a public debate on issues of national identity and tolerance.

Fiji

The year 2006 proved to be an eventful one for minority rights protection in Fiji. Despite the Fijian Labour Party, representing the large Indian minority (45 per cent), taking its place in a power-sharing system with the ethnic Fijian Soqosoqo Duavata ni Lewenivanua party, a military coup ousted the government on 5 December. The takeover – Fiji's fourth in two decades – was the culmination of a long impasse between coup leader Commodore Frank Bainimarama and Prime Minister Laisenia Qarase over attempts to offer pardons to conspirators in the 2000 coup and to grant lucrative coastal land ownership to indigenous Fijians. Commodore Bainimarama, himself an indigenous Fijian, said the bills were unfair to the island's ethnic Indian minority. At the time of writing, the island was enjoying a relative calm and the interim government was taking shape, with eight ministers being sworn in to work under Bainimarama who has been declared Prime Minister.

East Asia

Although many states vary in terms of their political structure and ideology, the need for specific minority rights standards is considered of low importance in East Asia or not accepted. China is a notable exception, however, enjoying a Constitution that enshrines minority rights and allows for ethnic autonomy in some of its regions. Nevertheless, the state's system of categorizing minorities is fraught with difficulties and, in reality, ethnic minorities suffer discrimination in all walks of life. China's relentless economic development appears to be overshadowing protection of rural ethnic communities, with forced migration from areas such as Inner Mongolia to urban centres being increasingly commonplace.

Japan and Mongolia have traditionally considered themselves to be ethnically homogeneous, resulting in either a lack of implementation or neglect of minority issues. Important exceptions to this rule in 2006 were the election of a Japanese parliamentary representative from the caste-based Okinawa community, and the provision of native-language education for ethnic Kazakh children in Mongolia.

People's Republic of China

The definition of ethnic minorities/nationalities in the People's Republic of China has been conceived by the state and does not truly reflect the self-identification of such ethnic minorities or the reality of ethnic diversity within China's boundaries. *Mínzú* (the Chinese term that signifies non-Han 'undistinguished ethnic groups', numbering more than 730,000 people) have not been recognized among or classified within the state's official 56 ethnic minorities (these comprise the majority Han grouping and 55 minority nationalities).

The *Mínzú* also do not include ethnicities that have been classified by the state authorities as belonging to existing minorities and hence denied their legal rights to public participation. For example, the Mosuo are officially classified as Naxi, and the Chuanqing are classified as Han Chinese, but they reject these classifications as they view themselves as separate ethnic minorities.

Some groups are still actively fighting for recognition as minorities. In the 1964 census, there were 183 nationalities registered, among which the government recognized only 54. However, census numbers are somewhat suspect due to the re-registration of significant numbers of Han people as members of minority nationalities in order to gain personal benefits, such as exemption from the family planning policy of 'one family one child' or the right to cremate their dead.

The recognized ethnic minorities have considerable autonomy with regard to their way of life and this has resulted in complicated forms of autonomy for six provinces (among them Inner Mongolia, Tibet and Xinjiang), but also in the creation of autonomous cities, prefectures and municipalities where minority nationalities are territorially concentrated. In practice, the system remains subject to the political control of the Communist Party. For instance, the Constitution stipulates that the leaders of an 'autonomous area', and most of its representatives to the People's Congress, must be members of the area's main nationality. However, the Chinese Communist Party, which controls the government and holds all final decision-making powers, is exempt from these stipulations. According to available records, appointments made in September 2006 to the Chinese Communist Party's committee in Lhasa, which in effect runs Tibet's capital, had a lower proportion of Tibetans than at any time in the last 40 years.

China's western regions are the most ethnically diverse, with 80 per cent of the country's minorities living in the area. However the *Mínzú* are mainly distributed in the border areas of the north-east, north, north-west and south-west of China. Many of these regions have significant natural resources, including oil, gas, minerals and precious metals, and new regional development strategies are being specifically targeted there. Nevertheless, without accompanying decentralization of political power, this strategy risks further exacerbating the already simmering ethno-regional tensions, as development rights for these groups are totally controlled by the central government.

Since 11 September 2001, the Chinese government claims to be acting against global terrorism. However, activists say that this is a convenient excuse to crack down on areas susceptible to ethnic tensions. This has led to widespread arbitrary arrests, closure of places of worship and the sentencing of hundreds of people to harsh prison terms or death after grossly unfair and often summary judicial processes. China's 8.68 million Uyghurs, who are the largest Muslim ethnic group in the country, have felt the brunt of these policies in 2006, particularly in Urumqi, the capital of the Xingiang Uighur Autonomous Region (XUAR). Uyghur observance of Islam is severely curtailed on a routine basis; mosques are under government control, and students and civil servants are not allowed to publicly engage in any religious activity other than observing the Muslim ban on eating pork.

According to the population census in 2000, the illiteracy of ethnic minorities is 14.63 per cent, 60 per cent higher than the national average. As such, a central government 2006 decision to allocate a special fund of 10 million *yuan* (US $1.28 million) each year to foster the education level of minorities and improve school conditions for primary and middle school students in minority areas is to be applauded. A *China View* (Xinhua news agency) article in November 2006 reports that about 6 million children are attending more than 10,000 bilingual schools in China, using both Mandarin and ethnic languages, and more than 3,000 textbooks are compiled in 29 languages annually.

Throughout 2006, the Chinese state continued investing to improve ethnic minorities TV programming in minorities' languages. Currently, in the autonomous areas of ethnic minorities, of 441 radio programmes, 105 are in ethnic minority languages. In addition, of 489 TV programmes, 100 are in ethnic minority languages. Moreover, the TV stations managed at prefecture or county level in ethnic areas also use more than 10 ethnic minority languages or dialects, including but not limited to Dai, Kazakh, Kirghiz, Korean, Mongolian, Tibetan, Uyghur and Zhuang.

Ethnic minorities find it increasingly difficult to compete for certain jobs; it is not uncommon to find signs at job fairs saying 'Uyghurs need not apply'. The huge boom in economic and industrial development in itself threatens the cultures and languages of minorities. China's famed Western Development Strategy exemplifies this trend, its main aim being to extract oil and gas from resource-rich rural areas for use in urban, coastal centres. Indirectly, however, Chinese Communist Party leaders hope that the resulting influx of Han Chinese settlers and state capital into the western regions will lead to assimilation in areas currently dominated by the presence of minorities. Ultimately, it appears to be an internal colonization project. On a more positive note, the Chinese government partnered with United Nations Development Programme (UNDP) in 2006 to attempt to lift ethnic minority groups out of poverty through developing cultural-based industries and tourism.

Central Asia

While most of the Central Asian Republics are multinational in composition, they vary from Turkmenistan, described as 85 per cent Turkmen, Tajikistan and Uzbekistan – both 80 per cent Tajik and Uzbek respectively, to Kyrgyzstan and Kazakhstan, where the majority is less dominant (around 60 per cent). Unlike some of the other former Soviet Republics in Europe, the relative homogeneity of each of the states means that there is a reduced possibility of ethnic conflict. Religious persecution is rife in all of the republics, however, both of Muslims who are considered 'extremists' and of minority faiths such as Baptists and Hare Krishna devotees.

Despite the establishment of modern constitutions replete with human rights standards and accession to several human rights treaties in the post-Soviet era, the states have a low level of compliance with international human rights standards, resulting in a lack of opportunities for women, especially those from minority communities. In addition, the need for the resource-rich states of the region to capitalize on their natural wealth has meant that development remains the top priority, and this is being implemented through increased urbanization.

In November 2006, Kazakhstan, Kyrgyzstan, Tajikistan and Uzbekistan decided to launch an inter-state dialogue and assist each other on issues of social integration and national minority education. A first working group meeting is scheduled to take place early 2007 and will be monitored by the Organization for Security and Cooperation in Europe (OSCE) High Commissioner on National Minorities.

Uzbekistan

In May 2005, the government responded to an armed uprising in Andijan, Uzbekistan, with indiscriminate force, gunning down hundreds of mostly unarmed civilians. The protest started when a group of armed people freed 23 businessmen accused of Islamic extremism and took officials hostage in local government buildings. Repercussions were felt throughout the region as refugees fleeing the violence flooded into Kazakhstan, Kyrgyzstan and Russia, some of whom were forcibly repatriated in blatant contravention of the 1951 Refugee Convention. Despite European Union (EU) sanctions imposed after the massacre, the crackdown on dissent among minorities in Uzbekistan has continued. In May 2006, the UN Special Rapporteur on Torture documented reports of torture, disappearances and harassment against Muslims who practise their faith outside state controls. Many are labelled terrorists, and have been convicted of religious extremism, yet the government continues to create conditions in which popular support for radical Islam is likely to grow. In October 2006, President Karimov fired Andijan governor Saydullo Begaliyev, naming him partially responsible for the Andijan massacre, but generally Karimov continues to deny that his

regime's policies were in any way at fault, while the same abuses go unchecked in other provinces.

State control of religious expression is extreme in Uzbekistan. In December 2006 Uzbekistan's state Religious Affairs Committee and state-controlled Spiritual Administration of Muslims (the Muftiate) restricted the number of Uzbek Muslims making the Haj pilgrimage to 5,000. According to Forum 18, a Norwegian non-governmental organization (NGO) reporting on threats against the religious freedoms of all people, on 24 September, a Baptist church in Tashkent was raided mid-way through a sermon and two church members subsequently fined, while on 1 October, in the town of Angren, nearly 50 members of a registered Pentecostal church were taken to the police station after their Sunday service was raided. Other religious minorities also face severe pressure. Forum 18 also reports that a Hare Krishna devotee was taken to the Khorezm police department on 19 August. Under pressure from her parents and officials from the law enforcement agencies, she signed a document renouncing her religious beliefs.

Kyrgyzstan

In Kyrgyzstan, ethnic Uzbeks form the largest national minority and are concentrated mainly in the southern and western parts of the country, especially the Ferghana Valley and the three administrative provinces of Batken, Osh and Jalal-Abad. The Uzbek language does not have any official status and this has indirectly led to the continued under-representation of Uzbeks employed in government offices. Demonstrations calling for official status for the language, and for some kind of proportional representation of Uzbeks in state administration in the southern provinces, have been held in 2006. A former governor of the Osh province alleged that President Bakiyev removed him from his position because of his Uzbek ethnicity. In October 2006, the head of the Center of Uzbek Culture in Osh was murdered and an investigation into his death remains unresolved.

The trend towards a 'Kyrgyzstan for the Kyrgyz' has gathered pace in 2006. New language provisions require that candidates for elected office need to demonstrate proficiency in Kyrgyz, as do students wishing to enter or graduate from university. State officials are to use primarily Kyrgyz, though Russian remains as a 'language of inter-ethnic communication'.

In February 2006, clashes between Kyrgyz and Dungan youth in a village about 70 km outside the capital, Bishkek, were feared by some to be a symptom of growing resentment and nationalism. The Dungans are Muslims of Chinese origin who moved to central Asia in the 1870s to escape persecution at home and there are about 40,000 in the country today.

Kazakhstan

Although religious minorities have been generally free to operate in Kazakhstan, in July 2005 President Nazarbaev signed 'amendments to laws relating to national security' making it compulsory to register all religious communities and banning the activities of all religious organizations that have not been registered. Attempts in 2006 to confiscate Hare Krishna devotees' property near Almaty could be justified under the new amendment.

On the positive side, Kazakhstan ratified two major human rights conventions in January 2006, the International Covenant on Civil and Political Rights and the International Covenant on Economic, Social and Cultural Rights. If implemented in domestic law, these could offer greater human rights protection for minority groups.

By 2006, the number of ethnic Germans in Kazakhstan appears to have fallen to about 200,000. While traditionally concentrated in the Akmola, Kostanai and North Kazakhstan areas, their remaining numbers now predominantly live in central Karaganda, and in the north and the east of Kazakhstan. The villages where Germans were mainly concentrated and the German language was used most frequently have been taken over by ethnic Kazakhs as their former inhabitants have mostly migrated *en masse*.

Tajikistan

The Tajiks are an Iranian people who speak a variety of Persian, an Indo-Aryan language. Most of them are Sunni Muslims and they make up about 80 per cent of the population of Tajikistan, according to an official 2000 census. The country is home to over 80 ethnic groups, most notably Kyrgyz, Russians, Tatars, Ukrainians and Uzbeks. Tensions between Uzbeks and Tajiks increased further in November 2006 after a Tajik border guard shot and killed an Uzbek counterpart. At the close of 2006, the government began resettling about 1,000 volunteer families,

purportedly to help create new farmland in the west of the country. However, observers note that virtually all of the families are ethnic Tajiks, while their new home is an area mainly populated by ethnic Uzbeks.

Tajikistan has tried to encourage Russians and Ukrainians to remain in the country, as many of them occupy technical and other skilled positions. For these reasons, schools teaching in Russian have been maintained and the Russian language is still in widespread use in government and business. Tajik legislation now permits dual citizenship but many Russians in Tajikistan still appear to want to leave because of the country's poor economic conditions.

Turkmenistan

Turkmenistan's notorious president Saparmurat Niyazov died at the end of December 2006, after 21 years of authoritarian rule of the Central Asian republic. This country is one of the most despotic of the region, with the tyrannical regime tolerating no opposition or freedom of the media. The one-party state was completely under the tight control of President Niyazov, who not only declared himself 'Turkmenbashi' (the father of all Turkmen), but was also made 'president-for-life' by the People's Council in 2003. His book on spirituality and morality – the Rukhnama ('Book of the Soul') – is compulsory reading in schools and workplaces, and is intended to help displace the Koran as the primary Turkmen religious guide (Turkmenistan is 90 per cent Muslim).

President Niyazov is reported to have called for the enhancement of the 'purity' of the Turkmen and for the removal of those who dilute Turkmenistan's 'blood'. While verifiable statistics and data are hard to come by given that NGOs – both domestic and international – cannot be based or operate in the country, anecdotal information and reports from observers confirm the continuing extensive exclusion of minorities (Russians and Uzbeks) from most areas of employment and participation in public life. Senior officials must be able to trace their Turkmen ancestry for several generations and it is reported that members of ethnic minorities are excluded from positions in the judicial system, law enforcement and military organizations.

Although the interim leader has pledged stability, Turkmenistan, which has large gas reserves, now faces an uncertain future with rival groups and outside powers scrambling for influence.

South Asia

The legal systems of the countries of South Asia have administrative, legislative and judicial measures for the protection of minority rights, and, in general, government policies demonstrate a willingness to tackle economic and social rights of minorities. India, however, highlights the importance of implementation of standards: while the state has a plethora of minority rights standards, minorities continue to be vulnerable. This phenomenon is manifest in long-standing secessionist conflicts in India, but also apparent in Sri Lanka, and, to a lesser extent, in Pakistan. The year 2006 saw the King of Nepal's dictatorial rule overturned by a movement of the masses and the government struggling to come to terms with the demands of Maoist insurgents. The warring factions finally signed a peace agreement in November 2006 and elections are promised for 2007. The re-building process in Afghanistan has struggled against persistent violence. NATO troops appear unable to restore order and face increasing attacks from Taliban forces. Even though the new Constitution passed in 2005 under the leadership of Hamid Karzai promises the protection and promotion of minority and women's rights, these can only ever be put into action if peace and stability return to the country. Afghanistan and Pakistan have also been in the frontline of the US and coalition forces' fight against international terrorism, with particularly dangerous consequences in Pakistan, where swathes of villages in the northern areas have been bombed.

India

India recognizes three types of minorities: religious, caste based and linguistic. According to the National Minorities Commission, the designated minority religions are Buddhists, Christians, Muslims, Sikhs and Zoroastrians. The Indian Constitution designates Scheduled Castes (SCs or Dalits, comprising 16 per cent of the population) and Scheduled Tribes (STs or Adivasis, 8 per cent of the population) for protection by enacting affirmative action programmes that provide not only equal protection in law but also 'reservation' of seats in the Assembly and national Parliament. An Act of Parliament passed in 1973 allows women and SCs and STs entitlement to 'reservation' jobs in government, educational institutions and elected

bodies. The government has established nearly 35 bodies for the protection of minorities at a national level, including the National Commission for Scheduled Castes, other Backward Castes, Minorities and Linguistic Minorities. Numerically large linguistic minorities with a distinctive history and regional identity, such as Gujaratis and Maharashtrans, have been entitled to a state-province within the Indian federation.

Evidence of continued commitment to minority rights standards in India in 2006 included the creation of a Ministry for Minority Affairs, the publishing of the *Sachar Report on the Social, Economic and Educational Status of the Muslim Community* and the Prime Minister's 15-point programme for the welfare of minorities. The government has also been considering a *Draft Plan for the Tribals*, however activists have criticized both the contents of the draft and the lack of adequate opportunity for consultation with leaders of Adivasi groups.

While Dalits and Adivasis have begun to mobilize themselves politically, they remain on the fringes of Indian society despite the affirmative action in their favour. An attempt to raise 'reservations' in public institutions to 50 per cent in April 2006 has divided the country. Meanwhile, Dalits and Adivasis continue to languish at the bottom of social indicators tables, face rising levels of discrimination and are often subject to violence. In September, in a village in the Bhandara district of Maharashtra, a Dalit woman and her three children were dragged out of their home by an upper-caste mob and murdered. The four were reportedly beaten with bicycle chains and sticks. The mother and daughter were allegedly raped by the mob, many of whom lived in the same village and were possibly their neighbours. The murders remain unresolved and Dalit organizations accuse state police of mishandling the case.

Frustrations with the oppression of the Hindu caste system continues, and is visible in mass ceremonies of Dalit conversions to both Buddhism and Christianity in 2006. However, if Dalits convert to Christianity and are then discriminated against, they will have no recourse to the protections and safeguards that exist for Buddhist, Hindu and Sikh Dalits.

India's 138 million Muslims (13.4 per cent) remain particularly vulnerable; 31 per cent of them fall below the poverty line, according to the Sachar report. The seeds of distrust against Muslims in

Left: A woman mourns her son, who was allegedly beaten to death in a police raid on their Adivasi tribal village in Bokaro, Jharkhand State, India. Police targeted members of the Adivasi community following the robbery of a jewellery store.
Robert Wallis/Panos Pictures

India go back at least to the battle for Indian independence and partition. The perceived grievances have been nursed through the conflict in Jammu and Kashmir, and more recently through the bomb-blasts on the Mumbai rail network on 11 July 2006, which claimed over 200 lives. Police claimed that the Mumbai attacks bore the hallmarks of an Islamic militant group. The investigations continue.

India's troubled north-east has also been marked by ethnic tension. Although fragile, the ceasefire between the Nationalist Socialist Council of Nagaland (NSCN) and the government remained in place and the rebels' cause was weakened by factional infighting. The NSCN believes that India should create a unified Naga homeland by merging the Naga-inhabited areas of Manipur, Assam and Arunachal Pradesh states into the state of Nagaland. Ever since talks between the United Liberation Front of Assam and the government collapsed in September 2006, the insurgents have targeted minority Hindi-speaking migrants, mostly from the northern state of Bihar, with bomb and grenade attacks. Fifty-five migrant workers were killed during the first days of 2007.

Pakistan

Pakistan has a large Muslim majority population (96.58 per cent), the bulk of whom are Sunni. There were simmering tensions between the majority Sunni and minority Shia Muslims. In February 2006 the violence came to the strategically important North West Frontier Province (NWFP) bordering Afghanistan. At least 31 people were killed and scores injured after a suicide bomber attacked a congregation of Shia Muslims marking the Ashura festival in Hangu. In May 2006, at least 57 people were killed, amongst them the entire leadership of the Sunni Tehrik group, in the suicide bombing of a congregation of Sunnis celebrating the Eid Milad festival in Karachi. According to Human Rights Watch, at least 4,000 people, largely from the Shia community, have died as a result of sectarian hostility since 1980.

In July 2005, the Provincial Assembly of the NWFP, led by the religious coalition MMA (Mutahida Majlis-e-Amal), voted in favour of the Hasba Bill, which establishes a Muhtasib (a person qualified to be a Federal Sharia Court judge) to monitor observance of Islamic and *Sharia* 'values'. The Supreme Court subsequently annulled the draft law because it was 'discriminatory'. However, in November 2006, the Provincial Assembly approved the bill with minor changes that they said took into account the Supreme Court's concerns. The bill has sparked protests by the APMA (All Pakistan Minorities Alliance), who, together with human rights organizations, are calling for its dissolution, claiming it seeks to 'Talibanize' both the NWFP and the country as a whole.

The Asia Human Rights Commission notes that it has become a common practice in Pakistan for Muslim seminaries to encourage young men to convert non-Muslim minorities to Islam. Young Hindu girls are usually kidnapped for this purpose but, when arrested by the police, their Muslim male kidnappers produce marriage certificates and evidence from Madrassas stating that the girls have adopted Islam. Many of these girls are minors but the courts appear to overlook this fact and simply accept the certificates as legitimate.

In Baluchistan, the head of the Bugti tribe was killed in an incident with the armed forces in August 2006 while hiding out in caves near his village, Dera Bugti. Baluchistan is the most economically marginalized province in Pakistan and he and his followers were demanding greater compensation from the government for exploitation of the natural gas reserves present on their lands. This killing caused huge riots across Baluchistan and in other parts of the country, and highlighted the unequal relations between the provinces and the centre.

The Hudood Ordinance, a set of laws enacted in 1979, makes rape victims in Pakistan liable to prosecution, and has led to thousands of women being imprisoned for so-called 'honour' crimes. The laws rendered most sexual assault victims unable to seek redress through the criminal justice system, deeming them guilty of illegal sex rather than victims of unlawful violence or abuse. The Hudood Ordinance has always provoked debate across the country, with members of the MMA religious coalition opposing any changes as 'un-Islamic' and all other parties and NGOs calling for a full repeal. In a small but important victory for women's rights, the National Assembly finally passed the November 2006 Women's Protection Bill, an amendment to the Hudood Ordinance. Although it still leaves many other discriminatory provisions in place, this amendment permits rape victims to file charges under the criminal law instead of the previous religious law (which required four male witnesses to guarantee proof of rape).

Sri Lanka

While in several of the states in this region there is simmering discontent and elements of ethnic tension, in Sri Lanka this has taken the shape of a full-scale civil war that has divided the island. The state's largest ethnic groups, the Sinhala (74 per cent) dominate state institutions and the army. Meanwhile the Liberation Tigers of Tamil Eelam (LTTE, drawn from the minority Tamil community – 13 per cent) have resorted to guerrilla warfare and have clashed with the Sri Lankan security forces in a decades-long armed confrontation.

The hope of the peace process yielding dividends was shattered in 2006 when the island was plunged back into a war reminiscent of the 1990s. Peace talks in Geneva in October 2006 were a failure, despite both sides claiming to adhere to the 2002 ceasefire. Nearly 3,000 people have been reported killed in the fighting in 2006, with 216,000 displaced.

In the context of this conflict, the 2 million-strong minority Muslim population is often ignored. In September 2006, civilians in Muttur in eastern Sri Lanka, a town with a large Muslim population, were caught in the crossfire as air force planes bombed LTTE targets, forcing residents to flee and seek shelter in overcrowded camps with poor sanitation. (See pp.18–24)

Nepal

In Nepal, after months of negotiations following the April 2006 mass movement that overturned King Gyanendra's direct rule, a peace agreement was signed on 21 November 2006 between Maoist insurgents and the government. The agreement ends a 10-year civil war and charts a course towards June 2007 elections for a Constituent Assembly following the formation of an interim government that includes the Maoists. Although all members of society have welcomed a cessation to the violence

and instability, Nepal's minorities claim that the peace agreement was drawn up without sufficient minority input and fear that the new constitution in 2007 will not bring them real change.

Careful reading of the agreement shows that it does not propose to alter electoral systems enshrined in the much-criticized 1990 Constitution. Nepal's *janajatis* (which include the 59 member organizations of the Nepal Federation of Ethnic and Indigenous Nationalities and the Indigenous Peace Commission) feel that the current system of constituencies and representation has always ignored their aspirations and as a result have little faith in the approaching June 2007 elections.

Being overwhelmingly Hindu (80.6 per cent), notions of caste within Nepalese society are deep-rooted and discrimination against the 2.8 million Dalits or 'untouchables' (13 per cent of the total population) remains rife. The peace agreement promises:

> *'to address the problems related to women, Dalit, indigenous people, Janajatis, Madheshi, oppressed, neglected, minorities and the backward by ending discrimination based on class, caste, language, sex, culture, religion, and region and to restructure the state on the basis of inclusiveness, democracy and progression by ending the present centralized and unitary structure of the state.'*

However Dalit organizations point out that, even though caste discrimination was outlawed in the 1963 and 1990 Constitutions, the legal provisions were never implemented. They argue that implementation of these promises would involve major structural changes and, up to now, they have seen no will by the entrenched political elite to relinquish their power. Yet another obstacle in the way of change is that enforcement of any new laws would mainly fall on the shoulders of the civilian police force who are traditionally unsympathetic to Dalit issues.

Bangladesh

Bangladesh is the world's third most populous Muslim nation and 2006 saw a growing campaign against religious minorities. The Ahmadiyya community, a revivalist movement within Islam originating in the Punjab in India and rejected by most mainstream Muslim sects, has continued to suffer in 2006. In June, 22 Ahmadi families living in Dhaka were publicly threatened with death by members of the Islamist group International Khatme Nabuwat, an organization dedicated to safeguarding the sanctity of the finality of the Prophet Mohammed. According to Amnesty International, by targeting the Ahmadiyya community Khatme Nabuwat is attempting to force the government to yield to their political demands for the introduction of more stringent Islamic law. They also hope to obtain mass support from poor and disenfranchised sections of society, whom they feel they could influence by appealing to their religious beliefs.

The tribal people of the Chittagong Hill Tracts (CHT) have for a long time been the targets of massacres and torture, notably during the years of armed conflict (mid-1970s to 1997). The signing of the peace accord between the government of Bangladesh and tribal representatives in December 1997 appeared to provide assurances that their rights would be respected. However, nine years later, the government has failed to implement fully some of the most crucial provisions of the accord. These include the rehabilitation of all returned refugees and internally displaced families, settlement of land confiscated from the tribal people during the conflict, withdrawal of non-permanent army camps from the CHT and transfer of power within the provisions of the peace accord to the local CHT administration.

The country is due to hold elections in 2007 – but the poll has already been postponed from the original date of 22 January. The run-up to the elections has already been marked by violence. NGOs warned that the rights of minorities to participate without fear and intimidation must be a priority.

Southeast Asia

Populations in Southeast Asia are characterized by large-scale migrations from China and India, in conjunction with dominant regional groups such as Malays and Indonesians (arguably both composite identities themselves), as well as a host of indigenous tribes and hill peoples. Islamic extremism has had a strong influence throughout the region in 2006, manifest in government crackdowns against militants in Muslim minority states or the installation of Sharia-inspired local laws in Muslim-dominated states such as Indonesia. Despite constitutional protections in both the Philippines and Malaysia, indigenous peoples have seen usurpation of their lands for commercial purposes continue to impact their struggle for greater land rights.

Thailand

The military coup in Thailand on 19 September 2006, was orchestrated by Thai Army Commander General Boonyaratglin during the brief absence of Prime Minister Thaksin Shinawatra. In October 2006, a new prime minister, Suayud Chulanont, and a new cabinet were installed – but the abrogation of the Constitution and the imposition of martial law has made it difficult to gauge the precise levels of support for this new arrangement.

The forging of a strong Thai nationality has always been given prominence over that of the ethnic Lao, who are numerically superior in Thailand. Other minorities, such as the Chinese, Indians, Khmer, Malays and Mon have been forced to adopt 'Thai' national identities in the name of building a unified state. This is most exemplified by the continuing armed violence in the Muslim Malay-majority southernmost provinces (Kala, Narathiwat and Pattani) where an estimated 1,750 people have died since January 2004. The origins of the violence lie in historical grievances stemming from discrimination and neglect of the local ethnic Malay Muslims, and attempts at forced assimilation by successive governments in Bangkok (dominated by Thailand's Buddhist majority – 94.6 per cent). Islamic militants have been fighting for the restoration of an independent Muslim sultanate in the region.

A National Reconciliation Commission was appointed in 2005 to consult with southern community and religious leaders about how best to address their grievances. In June 2006 they presented the government with a blueprint for policies to address the underlying cultural and economic grievances driving the insurgency, which was largely ignored. However, the new post-coup government has signalled a willingness to talk to the Islamic rebels and the people of the south are generally optimistic that their situation will now improve.

Indonesia

The last two years have seen a dramatic turnaround in the fortunes of Indonesia, the most populous Muslim-majority nation in the world. The country's first-ever direct presidential election, won by Susilo Bambang Yudhoyono in 2004 on a platform of reform and dismantling of the authoritarian state, has been followed by sustained progress on human rights. Democratic elections have been held at various levels and have served to dampen the ethnic tension that characterized the state for much of the 1990s. With policies of decentralization accompanied by devolved decision-making being offered (as manifest in the August 2005 peace agreement in Aceh), entrenched conflict appears to be ending.

Despite the Indonesian government's compliance with the Bush administration's counter-terrorism alliance, illustrated by the welcoming of President Bush by President Yudhoyono in November 2006, the visit was met with mass protest rallies across the country. There has been a revival in the representation of groups who have tried to bring in Islamic legislation in Indonesia: they have succeeded in garnering election victories through criticism of the corruption that still persists at every level of Indonesian society.

The rise of religious intolerance as manifest in attacks against Ahmadiyya mosques and Christian churches in Java and North Sumatra is indicative of the continued threat of Islamist extremists, and has already resulted in the installation of *Sharia*-inspired local laws in Aceh, Java, Sulawesi and Sumatra. Christian–Muslim tensions were particularly apparent in Sulawesi, where three Catholics, sentenced to death for their alleged role in the death of Muslims during religious riots, were executed in September 2006. Fearing outbreaks of violence, the Indonesian government deployed thousands of troops to protect Christian sites during the December 2006 Christmas celebrations.

In a radical shift from centuries of policies that favoured indigenous groups against Indonesia's Arabs, Chinese and Indians, the government passed a new citizenship law in 2006 in which 'indigenous' was redefined to include the ethnic Chinese population.

Burma

The November 2006 report of the UN Special Rapporteur for Burma highlights the deterioration in the rights, security and livelihoods of Burma's 54 million people. The repression of the ruling military junta against its population is most evident in attacks against minorities such as the Karen Hill Tribes. More than 10,000 Karen were displaced in a military attack by the junta in November 2006, with the prospects of them fleeing into Thailand to claim asylum being hindered by the presence of a large number of landmines on the Burmese side of the border. This latest attack by the military is the largest of its kind since 1997 and is resulting in a humanitarian disaster on a grand scale, with the tens of thousands of the displaced falling victim to water-borne diseases fuelled by Cyclone Mala. The systematic abuses are not restricted to the Karen, with ongoing conflicts against other ethnic minority rebel groups being waged, on the government side, through an array of extra-judicial executions, rapes, the use of torture and forced relocations of entire villages. Human Rights Watch estimates that, since the start of 2006, 232 villages have been destroyed in Burma as part of the army's campaign against ethnic insurgents, and 82,000 people have been forced to flee as a direct result of armed conflict. ■

Europe

Hugh Poulton

Racism, discrimination and intolerance remained prevalent throughout the 48 states of Europe. Apart from overt racism and discrimination, ethnic and national minorities face socio-economic exclusion and assimilation. Roma remain the most excluded and vulnerable group in Europe – closely followed by immigrants and some refugee groups – and face disadvantage in access to employment, education, housing and health care. Female members of minorities often suffer double or triple discrimination: as women, as members of minorities and as members of the poorest part of the population.

The admission of 10 new member states on 1 May 2004 saw the number ethnic minorities living in the previous 15-member European Union (EU) increasing from around 50 million to 80–100 million, not including immigrants. Only Ireland and the UK allowed free employment access to citizens of the new members. However, the large numbers of arrivals, especially from Poland, saw both Ireland and the UK announce in October 2006 that work permits would be needed for citizens of Bulgaria and Romania when they joined the EU in January 2007. In January 2006, the EU's European Monitoring Centre on Racism and Xenophobia (EUMC) published a comparative analysis, *Migrants, Minorities and Housing*, based on information supplied by the EUMC's national focal points. It shows that, across the EU, similar mechanisms of housing disadvantage and discrimination affect migrants and minorities, such as denial of access to accommodation on the grounds of the applicant's skin colour, imposition of restrictive conditions limiting access to public housing, or even violent physical attacks aimed at deterring minorities from settling in certain neighbourhoods. The report also documents instances of resistance on the part of public authorities to address such discrimination. In October 2006 the EUMC published a pilot study based on the data of 12 country studies of EU member states – Austria, Belgium, France, Germany, Greece, Ireland, Italy, Luxembourg, the Netherlands, Portugal, Spain and the UK. The study shows that a significant number of migrants in all 12 countries have subjectively experienced discriminatory practices in their everyday life.

The level of education among certain minority groups is generally low. Ethnic and national minorities experience language difficulties in state school systems resulting in high drop-out rates and even non-attendance. For example, the provincial government of Carinthia in Austria is openly anti-Slovene and has fought bitterly against the provision of Slovene education, with any student opting to do studies in Slovenian considered to be taking a political stand against the German-speaking establishment. Religious minorities in France continued to struggle with the impact of a 2004 law restricting the wearing of religious signs in the classroom. Although most attention has focused on the issues surrounding Muslim schoolgirls and the headscarf, in September 2006 four Sikh schoolboys were excluded from school for refusing to remove their turbans. In a separate case, a Sikh driver who was refused a replacement driving licence because his ID photo showed him wearing a turban, lost his appeal. The French authorities argued that the measure was taken on grounds of security and was not a restriction of freedom of religion. However, the French branch of United Sikhs said the case highlighted 'indirect discrimination' suffered by Sikhs.

The incentive of joining the EU has been used to pressure the 10 new members and the other applicant countries to improve their practices with regard to minorities. Most of these new member states have adopted higher legal standards on minority rights than the 15 member states. The key minority instrument of the 46-member Council of Europe (CoE) – Belarus and the new state of Montenegro are applicants – the 1995 Framework Convention for the Protection of National Minorities (FCNM) has not yet been ratified by a number of the CoE's members: Andorra, France, Monaco and Turkey have not signed the instrument, while Belgium, Greece, Iceland and Luxembourg and have signed but not ratified it. The new state of Montenegro ratified it in 2006. Some European countries continue not to recognize their minorities as such, clinging to a unified model of the homogenized state: e.g. France, Greece – which only recognizes religious minorities as laid down in the 1923 Treaty of Lausanne – and similarly Turkey, although there have been some recent changes in Turkey due to European pressure.

The rise of Islamophobia

The 11 September 2001 attacks in the USA, and the subsequent bombings in Madrid and London, have resulted in European governments – fearing further terrorist attacks – adopting legislation that curbs the rights of all citizens but predominantly

Left: A woman holds up the Koran as Muslim protesters demonstrate outside the Norwegian Parliament. Anger erupted around the Muslim world after the publication of a controversial series of cartoons depicting the Prophet Mohammed in a Danish newspaper, which were then reprinted in a small Norwegian magazine. Fredrik Naumann/Panos Pictures

targets Muslim communities. This has led to both a rise in Islamic radicalism in response to perceived racial discrimination as well as a rise in Islamophobia among majority populations. The latter has resulted in Muslim communities, particularly in Western Europe, increasingly feeling intimidated and persecuted. In November 2006, the Dutch government, in what was viewed as a pre-election gambit, proposed banning the wearing of face veils in the streets, public places, schools and courts. In Germany, Muslim women wearing headscarves are particularly vulnerable to racist attacks, and some non-Muslim schools enforce strict policies against the wearing of headscarves. In Belgium, the Flemish Region requires mosques to meet certain conditions for public funding: outside of Arabic rituals, Dutch must be used, there must be tolerance for women and homosexuals and no preaching of extremist ideas. These restrictions apply only to Islam. Anti-Muslim sentiment continued to be fuelled in Russia by the conflict in predominantly Muslim Chechnya, and in Serbia due to the situation in Kosovo, which has a large Muslim Albanian majority.

Denmark
In March 2006, Doudou Diène, United Nations Special Rapporteur on contemporary forms of racism, racial discrimination, xenophobia and related intolerance, referred to the recent controversial depictions of the Prophet Mohammed in Danish newspaper cartoons and the subsequent violent reactions in many countries. He said: 'the cartoons illustrated the increasing emergence of the racist and xenophobic currents in everyday life'. He also pointed to the political context in Denmark, where an extremist political party enjoyed 13 per cent of the vote and had formed part of the governing coalition, and stated that 'the development of Islamophobia or any racism and racial discrimination always took place in the context of the emergence of strong racist,

extremist political parties and a corresponding absence of reaction against such racism by the country's political leaders'. In March 2006, Denmark's Director of Public Prosecutions upheld the earlier decision not to press criminal charges against those responsible for the cartoons on the basis that the drawings were protected by legislation on freedom of speech and did not violate bans on racist and blasphemous speech. In retaliation, the Islamic Faith Community, an umbrella organization of 27 radical Muslim organizations in Denmark, is lodging a complaint against the state of Denmark with the Office of the United Nations High Commission for Human Rights (OHCHR) in Geneva.

Spain
In 2006, the Spanish government approved a new Statute of Autonomy for Catalonia, further expanding the region's autonomous powers and strengthening Catalan culture. The statute was approved by referendum in Catalonia on 18 June 2006. Due to its geographical position, Spain is a primary entry point for African migrants to Europe. In November 2006 it was reported that some 16,000 illegal immigrants from Africa had come to the Canary Isles in 2006, and Spain continued to be accused of abuse against African migrants and asylum seekers. In July 2006, three were killed when they tried to enter the Spanish enclaves of Ceuta and Melilla from Morocco, allegedly as a result of Spanish and Moroccan law enforcement officers using disproportionate and lethal force to prevent them entering; in 2005 at least 13 people were similarly killed. In October 2006, Amnesty International again expressed its concern about the allegations of ill-treatment and excessive use of force by the Spanish Civil Guard, including use of firearms and heavy rubber bullets at close range, when confronting migrants and asylum seekers attempting to climb over the fences into Ceuta and Melilla. Moreover, Amnesty asserted that, when people are intercepted by Spanish Civil Guards in the area between the two border fences, they are often immediately unlawfully expelled through one of the gates in the fence closest to Moroccan territory.

United Kingdom
In the UK, the debate over multiculturalism intensified as the repercussions from the 11 September 2001 attacks in the US and the 7 July

2005 bomb attacks in London continued to reverberate. Tensions between the government and the Muslim community flared when some prominent British Muslims blamed the UK Middle East policy for 'giving ammunition to extremists' – an analysis roundly rejected by the government. In a poll of UK Muslims published in July 2006, 13 per cent of those questioned believed that the British suicide bombers who carried out the 7 July 2005 attacks, 'could be regarded as martyrs'. A month later, the Secretary of State for Communities and Local Government, Ruth Kelly, announced the establishment of a Commission on Integration and Cohesion. In her speech setting out the terms of the Commission, Ms Kelly said, 'We have moved from a period of uniform consensus on the value of multiculturalism, to one where we can encourage that debate by questioning whether it is encouraging separateness.' According to the government, the aim of the Commission is to look at best practice around the UK, with a view to coming up with recommendations on measures which encourage the integration of minorities. The Commission is due to report in July 2007. The debate over the position of the Muslim community in the UK crystallized in the row over Muslim women wearing veils. The issue seized the headlines in October 2006, when a senior government minister, Jack Straw – the former Foreign Secretary and now Leader of the House of Commons – revealed that he asked Muslim women who came to visit him in his constituency office to consider removing their veils. Mr Straw – who represents a constituency with a high Muslim population – argued that 'the veil is a visible statement of separation and of difference'. Many government ministers – including the Prime Minister Tony Blair – supported his view. The row gathered pace, when a Muslim classroom assistant in north-east England was suspended for insisting on wearing a veil in school when male colleagues were present. Although a small proportion of the Muslim women in the UK elect to wear the veil, the issue became a focus for questions about broader Muslim integration. In the torrent of debate in newspapers, on radio and on television, it was clear that there was a diversity of opinion on the matter – UK Muslims themselves were divided as to whether it was appropriate to wear the veil in all settings and circumstances. In November, the classroom assistant, Aishah Azmi, was sacked by her school. Previously,

an employment tribunal ruled that Mrs Azmi had not been discriminated against, but had awarded her compensation for 'injury to her feelings'.

South-East Europe

In some countries of the former Yugoslavia, discrimination on ethnic grounds in areas such as employment and housing continues to block a durable and dignified return for many people displaced by the conflicts of the 1990s. However, there was some improvement concerning the issue of refugee returns, with the Sarajevo Process seeing Bosnia and Herzegovina, Croatia, Montenegro and Serbia beginning to work together with international partners on the issues, although some of the most sensitive issues have yet to be tackled.

Kosovo

In February 2007, the UN's special envoy, Martti Ahtisaari, presented his plans for Kosovo's future. Following the NATO-led war of 1999, which took control of Kosovo away from Serbia, the territory – with its majority Albanian population – remained an international protectorate under UN Security Council Resolution 1244. Mr Ahtisaari proposed that Kosovo be given limited independence, with international supervision. Under Ahtisaari's plan, the Serb minority would have guaranteed places in the local government and parliament, as well as representation in the police and civil service, and a special status for the Serbian Orthodox Church. However, MRG expressed concern that the needs of other smaller minorities – including the Roma and Turks – have been side-lined under the new proposals. These communities had effectively been marginalized from the UN discussions on the future of Kosovo. There are fears that if a new constitution is rushed through a matter of months, they would be excluded again.

The situation of minorities in Kosovo is perhaps the worst in Europe. Basic human rights including the right to life continue to be violated. People face harassment and physical violence for being who they are, for living in their homes if they belong to the 'wrong' community, or for speaking their own language. The authorities, thus far, have been unable or unwilling to bring those responsible for crimes to justice. This includes those responsible for ethnic cleansing after the establishment of the international protectorate in 1999 and again in Spring 2004. These waves of violence saw Kosovo's minority population diminish further and people forced to live in enclaves. Furthermore, segregation is institutionalized and discrimination in access to employment and public services such as health-care, is allowed to continue. MRG is extremely concerned that under the UN proposals, segregation will become even more deeply entrenched, and it will become even harder to translate the legal prohibition on discrimination into a practical reality on the ground.

Serbia

The UN proposals on Kosovo's future were badly received in Belgrade. Serbia's president stated flatly that his country would never accept the independence of Kosovo – many Serbs see the province as the cradle of their culture, with many important religious and cultural sites. Overall, the rise of virulent Serbian nationalism continued, with the January 2007 elections, seeing the nationalist Serbian Radical Party taking almost thirty per cent of the vote. The Radicals – which ran a campaign opposing EU membership and for a Greater Serbia – now form the biggest bloc in the Serbian parliament.

In the Vojvodina, which has a Serbian majority but which is an ethnic mosaic including a substantial Hungarian minority, reports of intimidation of Hungarian, Slovak and other minority communities continued in 2006, although there was a decrease in the number of incidents. The situation in Sandzak also remained tense between the majority Serb and the minority Bosniac communities. In April 2006, the Serbian government dissolved the municipal administration in Novi Pazar, heightening political tensions, which came to a head in September 2006 when a Bosniac candidate was killed during local elections. In October 2006 a referendum (criticized as being neither free nor fair) approved a new Constitution for Serbia, which curtailed human and minority rights, specifically in Articles 10, 20 and 114. Article 10 stipulated that the Serbian language and the Cyrillic script be used for official communications, while the use of 'other languages and scripts shall be regulated by law based on the Constitution', effectively banning them for official use until such laws are passed. The wording of Article 20 allows the government to curtail human and minority rights for unspecified reasons, while Article 114 requires the President 'to preserve the sovereignty and integrity of the territory of the Republic of Serbia,

including Kosovo and Metohija as its constituent part', thus making any recognition of independence for Kosovo constitutionally impossible.

Montenegro

The Union of Serbia and Montenegro ended with a referendum on 26 May 2006, when just over the required 55 per cent of Montenegrin citizens voted in favour of independence for Montenegro. It appears that most Montenegrins wanted to join the EU and were apparently dismayed at Belgrade's policies (e.g. harbouring war criminals, and its fixation on Kosovo) that inhibited progress toward accession. In April 2006, the Montenegrin Parliament adopted a new Law on Minority Rights and Freedoms, which provides for a general framework for the protection of minorities and affirms the multi-ethnic character of Montenegro and Montenegrin society. This includes non-discrimination against ethnic and other minorities, use of minority languages, free association and participation of minorities in public and social life. It also envisages the establishment of minority National Councils, as well as a Republican Fund for Minorities. However, a motion launched before the Constitutional Court questioned some provisions of the law providing for affirmative action in the area of elections and parliamentary representation of minorities through a guaranteed quota of seats, and the Constitutional Court annulled the related provisions.

Bosnia and Herzegovina

Bosnia and Herzegovina is made up of two Entities, the Republika Srpska and the Federation of Bosnia and Herzegovina. It is a state of three constituent peoples – Bosniacs, Croats and Serbs – and 'Others', which includes anyone who does not identify with one of the three ethnic groups, including all minorities, people of mixed ethnicity who do not wish to identify with one group over the others, and those who simply identify as Bosnian citizens. The term 'Others' is problematic as it implies exclusion. Important rights, such as the right to stand and vote for certain offices, including the House of Peoples and the three-person Presidency, are granted on the basis of ethnic belonging and not on the basis of citizenship. In January 2007, a leader of the Bosnian Jewish Community, Jakob Finci – supported by MRG – lodged an application with the European

Court of Human Rights in Strasbourg, challenging the discriminatory curtailment of these rights. The ethnically polarized campaigning during the elections of October 2006 reinforced this situation of ethnic discrimination. The Entity governments have far-reaching powers, while the power of the state government is very limited, although central government has gradually taken additional powers. Such an arrangement sets up a society where all citizens are not equal and people are discriminated against solely on the basis of their ethnicity. A July 2000 Decision of the Constitutional Court of Bosnia and Herzegovina states that Bosniacs, Croats and Serbs have the status of constituent peoples across the whole state, not just in the Entity where they form a numerical majority, i.e. Serbs in Republika Srpska and Bosniacs and Croats in the Federation. However, in practice there is widespread discrimination in the fields of public participation, employment, public services such as health care and pensions, and education, against minorities and constituent peoples living in areas where they are not the majority.

Macedonia

In Macedonia, ethnic Albanian political parties have been members of the governing coalitions since independence, and, in the run-up to the July 2006 elections, there were clashes between the two main Albanian political parties, the Democratic Union for Integration, which was in government, and the Democratic Party of Albanians (PDA). The elections saw the PDA joining the government coalition led by the previous opposition ethnic Macedonian party. The Commission of the European Communites, in November 2006, reported on Macedonia's accession to the EU and noted that '[i]n general, inter-ethnic relations have continued to improve. The commitment of the government to make progress in the implementation of the Ohrid Framework Agreement remained essential for the country's stability. Inter-ethnic issues were not conflicting issues during the electoral campaign.' The Ohrid Framework Agreement, which ended the armed conflict in 2001, provides for a range of legislative and policy measures to ensure equality and minority protection. As a result, constitutional changes have been made and legislation introduced or amended, including a decentralization law, giving official status to a minority language where at least 20 per cent of the population speak it, proportional representation, measures in education, as well as measures aimed at improved participation and employment of minorities in public life and state institutions. At the municipal level, Committees for Inter-ethnic Relations are being established in areas with more than 20 per cent minority population; if given a proper role, these could be an important mechanism for participation. The Ohrid Framework Agreement focuses on the ethnic Albanian and Macedonian communities, marginalizing smaller minority communities. While comprehensive legislative changes have been made, implementation of the laws, policies and programmes has varied, with progress in some but not in other areas.

The Russian Federation

Racism and xenophobia remain rife throughout Russia. In 2006, local and international media reported racist attacks – which have been taking place for years (in 2005 alone there were at least 28 racially motivated murders) – on an almost daily basis. In a report of May 2006, Amnesty International stated that racist attacks and killings of foreigners and members of ethnic minorities were being reported with 'shocking regularity' and 'disturbingly, their frequency seems to be increasing'. Victims included: students; asylum seekers and refugees from Africa and Asia; people from the south Caucasus; people from South, South-East and Central Asia; people from the Middle East and from Latin America; citizens of the Russian Federation who do not look typically ethnic Russian, such as ethnic groups of the north Caucasus, in particular Chechens, as well as members of the Jewish community, Roma and children of mixed parentage. Even ethnic Russians who are seen as sympathizing with foreigners or ethnic minority groups, for example fans of rap or reggae music, members of other youth subcultures and campaigners against racism, have also been targeted as they are perceived as 'unpatriotic' or 'traitors'. Attacks have been reported in towns and cities across the Russian Federation. Cases included the murder in March 2006 of a 70-year-old Afro-Cuban man working as a chef in a Moscow restaurant; the stabbing to death of Ainur Bulekbaeva from Kazakhstan in February 2006; the fatal shooting in April 2006 of Senegalese student Lamsar Samba Sell in St Petersburg, after a gunman opened fire on a group of foreign students as they left a weekly gathering of intercultural friendship between Russians and foreigners. In January 2006, nine people were stabbed at a Moscow synagogue by a man described as a 'skinhead'. People have been seriously injured in many other racist attacks.

Russian human rights activists claim that skinhead gangs operate under conditions of broad impunity, and have raised concerns regarding possible links between the Kremlin-sponsored 'youth movement' *Nashi* ('Our People') and xenophobic gangs. Human rights organizations believe that local authorities' silent endorsement of violent racism has fostered a climate of impunity for those perpetrating such attacks, with redress for victims of such attacks being minimal or non-existent. In April 2006, the Culture Minister of Kabardino-Balkaria (a Russian republic in the north Caucasus), Zaur Tutov, was attacked in Moscow, and witnesses made statements that the attackers had shouted racist slogans, such as 'Russia is for Russians!', during the assault, which resulted in Zaur Tutov being hospitalized with a fractured cheekbone, concussion and bruises. The Ombudsperson for Human Rights, Vladimir Lukin, following the initial failure of the Moscow procurator's office to classify the assault as racist, accused law enforcement officers of covering up the extent of racist violence.

The Russian Federation (RF) inherited the complex Soviet system of recognizing minorities with a territorial base. By January 1993, the politics of ethno-regionalism had produced a situation in which the Russian central authorities had recognized the special nature of most ethnic-based administrative units within the RF. Republican status (the highest) had been reached by 21 units, leaving a number of other units – six *krais*, 49 *oblasts*, one autonomous *oblast* and 10 autonomous *okrugs*. Since the demise of the Soviet system, the north Caucasus has emerged as the most ethnically volatile region in the RF. The area is riven with territorial and border disputes, involving many of the more than 60 distinct national, ethnic and religious groups (Christian and Muslim) in the region. In response to the new challenges that have faced the peoples of the region, a number of initiatives to create organizations to challenge Moscow's control have been launched, most notably in Chechnya. In the RF as a whole, the ambiguous and often contradictory rights allocated to the ethnic republics in the main agreements regulating

centre–regional relations have further reinforced the pyramid of inequality that has developed among minorities in the RF. Those minorities with their own officially recognized territory ('homeland') usually enjoy considerable advantages over other minority populations in the RF. However, the titular groups of autonomous areas with high concentrations of Slavic settlers have often faced problems similar to those of minorities lacking a formal homeland.

Chechnya remains a 'black hole' of massive human rights violations and abuses, accompanied by a lack of will by the Russian authorities to negotiate, although for most Chechens the climate has improved from the widespread terror of five years ago, when there were widespread abuses, including murder, kidnap and rape, by federal soldiers. In 2006, it was alleged that mostly fighters and their families were targeted. In November 2006, a report by the US-based non-governmental organization (NGO) Human Rights Watch concluded that torture and ill-treatment of suspected rebels in Chechnya was 'systematic', and that relatives of fighters had been kidnapped to discourage opposition. In November 2006, the European Court of Human Rights ruled that the Russian authorities had violated the right to life, liberty and security of Chechens Said-Khusein and Said-Magomed Imakaev (or Imakayev), and Nura Said-Aliyevna Luluyeva, and had failed to effectively investigate their subsequent 'disappearances' in 2000. The European Court of Human Rights found that the applicants, who were relatives of the 'disappeared', were subjected to inhuman and degrading treatment and that, in the Imakaev case, the applicant's right to private and family life had been violated. The European Court of Human Rights also criticized the Russian authorities in this case for failing to cooperate with the Court by not submitting relevant documents.

Turkey

Turkey, while having made notable progress in the last few years due to European pressure, continues to experience a major national identity problem with regard to recognizing minorities as well as facing up to its past history of repression against minorities such as the Armenians and the Kurds. Amid growing uncertainty about EU membership, the European Commission issued its annual progress report in November 2006, charting the country's progress towards accession. While noting some progress in

reforms, the Commission noted that there was 'a need for Turkey to address the serious economic and social problems in the South-East and to ensure full enjoyment of rights and freedoms by the Kurdish population'. In addition, apart from ensuring freedom of expression by amending Article 301 of the Penal Code and by bringing the legislation as a whole into line with European standards, further efforts were needed to strengthen freedom of religion, women's rights and minority rights. Article 301 of the Turkish penal code criminalizes the 'public denigration' of Turkishness, the Turkish Republic, the Grand National Assembly, the government, judiciary, military and security services in terms so broad as to be applicable to a wide range of critical opinions. More than 60 writers have been charged under the law since its introduction in 2005. For example, in September 2006 the novelist Elif Shafak was tried for 'insult' to Turkishness under Article 301 for comments referring to the Armenian massacres as genocide made by fictitious characters in her bestselling novel *Baba ve Pic* ('Father and Bastard'). The case provoked international condemnation and she was acquitted. Turkey's continuing refusal to admit to any notion of the Armenian genocide was highlighted by the EU Parliament report on Turkey of September 2006 and, in October, the French lower house of parliament passed a bill making it a crime to deny that Armenians suffered genocide at the hands of Ottoman Turks, provoking a furious reaction from Turkey. In January 2007, the Turkish-Armenian journalist and editor, Hrant Dink, who campaigned courageously for the public acknowledgement of the fate of Ottoman Armenians, was shot dead in an Istanbul street. His murder caused an international – and national – outcry, and prompted much soul-searching about the ugly rise in nationalism in Turkey. A youth from Trabzon was arrested for Dink's murder.

Minority Rights Group International (MRG) also continued to campaign for the rights of the hundreds of thousands of people displaced by the war in the south-east of the country. Many now live in poverty around Istanbul and other Turkish cities. Spurred by the accession criteria, the Turkish government

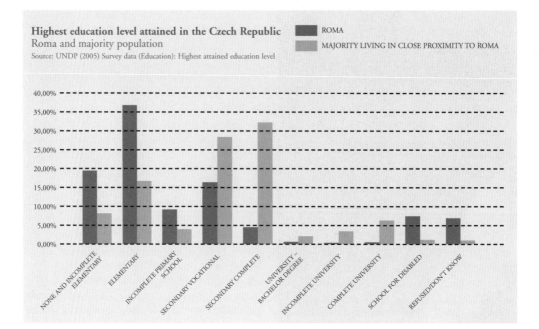

Highest education level attained in the Czech Republic
Roma and majority population
Source: UNDP (2005) Survey data (Education): Highest attained education level

ROMA
MAJORITY LIVING IN CLOSE PROXIMITY TO ROMA

introduced a new law to compensate for destroyed property. However, the authorities did not make strenuous efforts to inform those who may benefit from the laws – and the expiry date for compensation at the beginning of January 2007 passed with many still unaware of their new rights. When Pope Benedict XVI paid a landmark visit to Turkey in November 2006, issues of religious freedom once again came to the fore. Although Turkey is a constitutionally secular state that guarantees substantial rights to religious minorities, in practice deep-seated discrimination persists against non-Muslim minorities such as Christians and Jews, and Muslim minorities such as the Alevis – a Muslim sect different from Turkey's majority Sunnis, numbering 12–15 million. Despite changes to the law, adherents of minority religions continue to face discrimination in education, and over rights to own and establish places of worship in Turkey.

Roma

Across the region, Roma remain severely disadvantaged in key areas of public and private life, such as housing, employment, education and health services. They are also frequently the targets of racism by law enforcement officials and non-governmental actors. In April 2006, a group of 20 youths armed with metal bars and spades attacked a Roma family

and a visiting ethnic Russian woman as the group were sitting round a fire talking in the Volgograd region; a Roma man and the ethnic Russian woman were killed and others were seriously injured. On 24 January 2006, the European Roma Rights Center (ERRC) filed an application with the European Court of Human Rights against Romania, concerning a case of excessive and unjustified use of force by the police against the Roma Pandeles family in Targu Frumos in August 2003, as well as the subsequent failure of the authorities to conduct an effective investigation into the alleged incidents. In November, the Commission of the European Communities noted that Roma in Macedonia were still disproportionately the subject of ill-treatment by the police.

In April 2006, the EU Parliament released a report on the situation of Roma women in the EU, which stated that 'Romani women face extreme levels of discrimination including multiple or compound discrimination' and that they tended to have shorter life expectancy that other EU females; were often excluded from health care; faced attacks on their physical integrity, including coercive sterilization; often failed to complete primary education, and that Roma girls, along with Roma boys, faced racial segregation and biased attitudes from teachers and school administrators; were especially vulnerable to high unemployment; were frequently victims of trafficking; and that a significant proportion of Roma women (and men) throughout Europe lived in sub-standard housing.

Coercive sterilization of Roma women continued to be an issue in the Czech Republic and Slovakia, with no action by either government to provide adequate remedy to victims or even to comprehensively stop the practice. In August 2006, the UN Committee on the Elimination of Discrimination against Women (CEDAW) expressed its concern regarding coercive sterilization of Roma women by Czech doctors, as well as condemning Hungary for sterilizing a Roma women without her consent in January 2001. In August 2004, eight of the Roma women involved in sterilization cases filed a case with the European Court of Human Rights when Slovak hospitals allegedly denied them access to their own medical records. The case was ongoing at the time of writing.

Roma remain politically under-represented and Roma women especially so. In 2006, there were two Roma women from Hungary in the European Parliament, but there are none currently serving in any European national parliament, and representation of Roma women at the local level is similarly weak.

Roma children remained disadvantaged in access to education. In May 2006, the EUMC released a report, *Roma and Travellers in Public Education*, on the situation of Roma and Travellers in education across the EU, which showed that Roma and Traveller pupils are subject to direct and systemic discrimination and exclusion in education. In November 2006, Amnesty International released a report highlighting the lack of access of Roma children to primary education in Bosnia and Herzegovina, Croatia and Slovenia. The report noted that often Roma did not attend school, or did so only intermittently, and that many failed to complete even primary education; in places they were segregated in 'Roma only' groups or classes, where they are offered only a reduced curriculum; and racist attitudes and prejudice were prevalent, even among some teachers and educators working with Roma children. Such segregation in education is compounded in countries such as Serbia and Slovakia by dubious testing processes, whereby many Roma children are classified as educationally backward and sent to special schools. In May 2006, 18 Roma children forced to attend segregated

schools in the Czech Republic filed their final appeal before the European Court of Human Rights: in February 2006, the Court had ruled that, although the Roma children suffered from a pattern of adverse treatment, the Czech government's intent to discriminate was not proven.

Roma were the victims of forced evictions in a number of countries throughout 2006, including Bulgaria, Italy, Romania, Russia and Turkey. In October 2006, an extended Roma family was forced to leave their home in Ambrus in Slovakia by local inhabitants. In April 2006, the European Committee of Social Rights ruled that Italy, in both policy and practice, systemically violated Roma's right to adequate housing. The Committee ruled that: housing arrangements for Roma in Italy deliberately aimed at separating Roma from the mainstream of Italian society, thus blocking possibilities for integration and subjecting Roma to racial segregation; in a number of Roma settlements in Italy, housing conditions were so inadequate as to threaten the health and even the lives of the inhabitants; the Italian authorities regularly and systematically subjected Roma to forced evictions, arbitrarily destroying their property and humiliating the evictees; in many cases, those evicted became homeless; in some instances Roma evictees have been collectively expelled from Italy; and that a significant number of Roma in Italy lived under constant threat of forced eviction.

An important development is the Decade of Roma Inclusion, set to run from 2005 to 2015, which was initiated by the World Bank, the Open Society Institute and the Hungarian government in summer 2003. The Decade has four priority areas: education, employment, health and housing, and two cross-cutting areas, gender and non-discrimination. The governments of Bulgaria, Croatia, the Czech Republic, Hungary, Macedonia, Romania, Serbia and Montenegro, and Slovakia have signed up to the Decade's action plan. There is also the Roma Education Fund, which covers the same countries for the same time period. The potential of the Decade initiatives for improving the lives of the Roma is substantial. To date, however, the record of the participating countries on moving toward the stated goals has been mixed, with problems of insufficient resources allocated at national level, and with adequate participation of

Roma, which is often hampered by numerous internal divisions and rivalries, in the designing, drafting and implementation of plans.

In Bulgaria, a programme for Roma literacy and occupational training 'From Social Aid to Employment' was launched in May 2006, aiming to provide basic occupational training for unemployed Roma, and other measures were implemented in 2006 in line with the Decade of Roma Inclusion. However, the Commission of the European Communities in November 2006 noted that concerns persisted: measures to integrate Roma children in schools needed to be further enhanced to cover higher education; the health conditions of many Roma remained poor, with outbreaks of disease caused by poverty or lack of hygiene frequent, and many Roma continued to have limited access to health-care services; there was a need for greater access of Roma to the labour market; and that the forced evictions of non-registered Roma settlements were increasing tensions.

In Romania the new National Employment Plan, approved in August 2006, provided targeted action for minorities, including Roma, and the administrative capacity of the National Agency for Roma improved in 2006 as regional offices were being developed. However, implementation is slow and the social inclusion of the Roma remains a problem; overall living conditions are still inadequate; unemployment of Roma remains high; and forced evictions continue.

In Albania, the Commission of the European Communities noted in November 2006 that the disparity between the social and economic situation of Roma and that of the rest of the population was increasing, with 78 per cent of the Roma living in poverty and 39 per cent in extreme poverty. The situation of the Roma community in Tirana notably worsened in 2006, with some 40,000 Roma in need of social and economic support by November 2006. Only 12 per cent of the Roma are enrolled in secondary school, compared to a national average of 81 per cent. Social factors and the mobility of certain groups make lack of access to education and health services, especially vaccination, a particular problem. Weak or non-existent birth registration of Roma children in Albania, as well as lack of personal documents, makes them particularly vulnerable to human trafficking.

Denial of citizenship

Minorities in some countries continue to face discrimination around issues of their legal status. In Slovenia, thousands of people 'erased' in 1992 from the registry of permanent residents, mainly people from other former Yugoslav republics (many of them Roma), are still waiting for their status to be resolved. As a result of the 'erasure', many are denied full access to their economic and social rights. In Macedonia, one of the conditions for citizenship is to have a permanent source of income. This indirectly affects minorities, as they form a significant portion of the unemployed population, particularly Roma and Turks. Also, an applicant has to prove that they have continuously resided in Macedonia for eight years, and people often find this difficult to prove. The Ministry of Internal Affairs is often discriminatory towards Muslim minorities (Albanians, Bosniacs, Turks), who often find that they are denied citizenship on the grounds that they are 'unsuitable … due to security reasons'. Meskhetians in the Krasnodar Territory in Russia continue to be refused recognition of their citizenship on ethnic grounds and so are unable to access a wide range of basic rights. In Greece, the authorities still refused to reissue citizenship documents to some members of the Muslim population in western Thrace, with those affected thereby denied access to state benefits and institutions. In Estonia, in February 2006, the Council of Europe's Committee of Ministers noted that the number of persons without citizenship in the country was still disconcertingly high, while in Latvia, which similarly has strict citizenship criteria – including five years of permanent residence, command of the Latvian language, knowledge of Latvian history and Constitution, legal source of income, renunciation of previous citizenship and a pledge of loyalty to Latvia – as of January 2006, 80.1 per cent of the total population of Latvia were citizens, 18.3 per cent were non-citizens and 1.6 per cent aliens and stateless persons. Russians accounted for 66.5 per cent of the non-citizens. The continuing division of Cyprus has resulted in considerable numbers of people not yet afforded legal citizenship. ∎

Middle East

Eric Witte

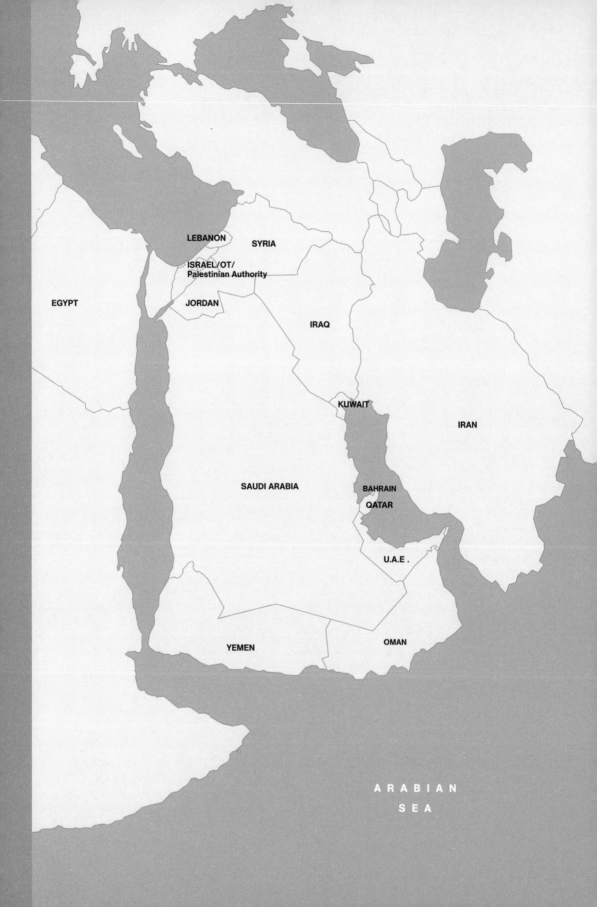

LEBANON

SYRIA

ISRAEL/OT/
Palestinian Authority

EGYPT

JORDAN

IRAQ

KUWAIT

IRAN

SAUDI ARABIA

BAHRAIN

QATAR

U.A.E .

YEMEN

OMAN

ARABIAN
SEA

The year 2006 was another year of conflict in the Middle East, marked by a worsening of sectarian and ethnic strife in Iraq; an intensive, month-long war between Israel and Hezbollah that saw widespread destruction in Lebanon; and continuation of the Israeli–Palestinian conflict. All of this violence had dire consequences for minority rights.

The Iraq Study Group commissioned by the US Congress warned in December 2006 of a 'broader regional war' fuelled by Sunni–Shia violence spilling out of Iraq. Indeed, Iran, Lebanon and Syria all saw a worsening of sectarian relations. Even in usually calm Bahrain, sectarian friction between the ruling Sunni minority and the 60 per cent majority Shia population rose ahead of November parliamentary elections, following the leaking of a government report in September that described the proposals of a government minister to weaken the Shia, including through election manipulation.

The Iraq war also sharpened the plight of Palestinian refugees trying to escape from Iraq without travel documents. As violence in Iraq escalated in 2006, Syria and Jordan both demonstrated reluctance to admit Palestinians camped at their borders. Minority women in Iraq faced the triple threat of targeting on the basis of religion, ethnicity and gender.

Iraq

Violence in Iraq continues to worsen, with a study in the *Lancet* finding that – as of September 2006 – the Iraqi death toll attributable to conflict since the March 2003 American-led invasion had risen to over 650,000. With mounting chaos, the United Nations (UN) estimated that, by October 2006, over 1.6 million Iraqis had fled the country and 100,000 more each month were abandoning their burning homeland. Militants sought to extend their control over land, principally by killing and expelling minority populations. Religious and ethnic minorities throughout Iraq became even more imperilled with acceleration of the cycle of killings and retribution, especially in sectarian violence between Shia and Sunni Arabs. Minority women faced added danger of violence from Islamic extremists, and even their own families, through so-called 'honour killings' following sexual violence. Some have stopped attending university in order to avoid coercion.

Muslims make up about 96 per cent of the Iraqi population. This overwhelming majority is mainly divided into a large Shia Arab majority, a Sunni Arab minority estimated at around 20 per cent, and around 6 million ethnic Kurds, who are mostly Sunni. An estimated 10 per cent of the population is not Shia Arab, Sunni Arab or Sunni Kurd, and includes ethnic Shabaks, Turkomans and Faili (Shia) Kurds, as well as Christians, Mandean-Sabeans, Yezidis and Baha'is.

The Baathist regime of former dictator Saddam Hussein was firmly based in the favoured Sunni Arab minority and became notorious for the repression and even slaughter of Shia, Kurds and many of Iraq's smaller minorities. Following the ouster of Saddam in 2003, the American-led occupying force installed a transitional government using ethnic and sectarian quotas that left Sunni Arabs feeling under-represented. Elections in January 2005, boycotted by Sunni Arabs, led to establishment of a government dominated by Shia and Kurds. This government oversaw the drafting and ratification of a new constitution in October 2005 that left Sunni Arabs feeling marginalized. Other minorities were also largely excluded from the process, as Western powers concentrated on forging consensus among the three main ethnic/sectarian groups, to which all but five of the 71 constitutional framers belonged.

The Shia Arab majority appeared content to await the post-Saddam transition that would cede them control of the country, and refrained from large-scale retaliation against Sunni Arab attacks until coming to power in the January 2005 elections. But, following those elections, Shia militants associated with the Iranian-backed Supreme Council for the Islamic Revolution in Iraq (SCIRI) and its Badr Organization, played a major role in the Interior Ministry and committed numerous indiscriminate attacks on Sunni civilians. In November 2005, US forces discovered an underground detention and torture facility run by the Interior Ministry in Baghdad.

Amidst this bloodshed, sectarian and ethnic division marked the campaign ahead of another round of elections in December 2005. The government arising from that vote is divided among the three main factions: President Jalal Talabani is Kurdish, Vice-President Tariq al-Hashemi is Sunni Arab, and Prime Minister Nuri Kamal al-Maliki is

Shia Arab; yet this power-sharing has not hindered Iraq's slide into sectarian civil war and dark days for its minorities.

Rival political parties within government openly support different militias who patrol various parts of the country in the name of community protection, but are also clearly working to extend their areas of control. These same militias detain, torture and conduct 'trials' of their victims, and summarily execute them with impunity. For example, Prime Minister Maliki depends on a faction allied with radical Shia cleric Moqtada al-Sadr. Many Sunni Arab victims of militia assaults report that perpetrators are in police or sometimes army uniforms, use police vehicles and act without interference from local police. Sunni Arab militants have targeted police stations and police recruits in retaliation for Shia Arab militia attacks, and to discourage cooperation with the government and international troops.

It is unclear to what extent Sunni Arab attacks are the work of domestic Baathist forces, or that of foreign insurgents, but it is increasingly clear that Iraqi Sunnis are engaging in sectarian violence. Shia militias have been unwilling to disarm because they say their community would then be endangered by the Sunni insurgency, but these in turn encourage Sunni Arab militancy. Iraqis of many stripes feel increasingly reliant on sectarian and ethnic militias because the American-led international and Iraqi government forces have proved incapable of establishing security.

The 22 February 2006 bombing of a Shia shrine set off a particularly fierce round of sectarian violence, the worst of which came in such mixed Sunni–Shia Arab areas of the country as Baghdad, Tal Afar and Diyala. The violence escalated throughout the year. Iraqi government figures placed the number of civilian dead for September and October 2006 at 7,054, with 5,000 of these killings in Baghdad. Most victims had been tortured. In one October incident, following the abduction and decapitation of 17 Shia civilians in the mixed Sunni–Shia Arab town of Balad, up to 90 Sunni civilians suffered reprisal killings and the UN Assistance Mission for Iraq (UNAMI) reported that most remaining Sunnis had fled the town. By November 2006, the UN estimated that 425,000 Iraqis had been displaced in sectarian violence since the February Samarra bombings. On 23 November,

a new assault threatened to intensify the killing further, as a series of car bombs, mortar attacks and rockets killed over 200 civilians in Sadr City, the Shia Arab slum of Baghdad and stronghold of leading Shia cleric Moqtada al-Sadr's Mahdi Army militia. In the aftermath, Shia Arab militants launched retaliatory attacks on Sunni civilians and their holy sites.

In September 2006 the International Organization for Migration (IOM) reported patterns of displacement that reflected the perceived threat to Shia and Sunni Arabs living as sectarian minorities. Shia Arabs were fleeing the Sunni Arab-dominated central Iraqi governates of Anbar and Salah al Din, as well as the mixed governate of Baghdad for the majority Shia Arab southern governates, while Sunni Arabs were moving from those southern governates into the governates of Baghdad, Diyala and Anbar. IOM also reported high rates of movement by Shia and Sunni Arabs into segregated towns and neighbourhoods within the mixed governates of Baghdad and Diyala.

The overwhelming reality of daily sectarian violence has left Iraq's smaller minorities particularly vulnerable. A report for Minority Rights Group International (MRG), published in early 2007, warned that the impact of the conflict on some minority groups has been so acute that they are in danger of being driven out entirely from a territory they have called home for hundreds – in some cases, thousands – of years. They are targeted on sectarian and/or ethnic grounds, and face added danger from the perception that they cooperate with American-led forces.

Iraq's ethnic Kurdish minority is mostly Sunni and concentrated in the north. Iraqi Kurds suffered greatly under Saddam's rule, but gained wide autonomy and relative prosperity during the sanctions regime, and with the Western air protection from Saddam's forces that preceded the 2003 invasion. Kurds in Iraq strive for greater autonomy and the dream of an independent Kurdistan, which is anathema to Iran, Syria and Turkey, all of which have neighbouring Kurdish minorities who, they fear, would seek to join such a new state. In July 2006, the International Crisis Group warned of a brewing battle for oil-rich Kirkuk in the north, which lies beyond the Erbil-based Kurdistan Regional Government's (KRG's) reach, but within its desire. Kurds used their position in the government elected in January 2005 to secure a process that would reverse the Saddam-era process of Arabization in Kirkuk, moving toward its eventual formal inclusion in the Kurdish region by referendum in late 2007. Turkey has signalled its opposition, as have Iraq's Sunni and Shia Arabs. Similarly, the Kurdish government in Erbil governate has attempted to extend its influence to the likewise disputed city of Mosul. In October 2006, a Kurdish member of parliament and his driver, who had been kidnapped earlier, were found dead – the suspected work of a Shia Arab militia. That same month, a senior member of the Patriotic Union of Kurdistan was assassinated in Mosul.

Kurdish claims on Kirkuk and Mosul clash with those of the Turkish-speaking Turkomans, Iraq's third-largest ethnic group, which makes up 3 per cent of the population, and has both Sunni and Shia adherents. Turkomans view Kirkuk as historically theirs and, with Turkish assistance, have formed the Iraqi Turkman Front (ITF) to prevent Kurdish control of Kirkuk. UN reports in 2006 indicated that forces of the KRG and Kurdish militias were policing illegally in Kirkuk and other disputed areas. These militas have abducted Turkomans and Arabs, subjecting them to torture. In June, 20 Turkoman students were killed in Kara Teppe and explosions in Turkoman areas of Kirkuk killed 13. A car bomb at a July parade by the ITF in Kirkuk wounded another 20. Turkomans also remain prone to predominant sectarian violence. Of 17 Turkoman officials arrested in October at a militia checkpoint in Tikrit, two Sunnis were released while 15 Shias disappeared.

The small ethnic Shabak minority, among which are both Sunni and Shia, has lived in the Nineveh Plains of the north for hundreds of years, but faces harassment from Kurdish militants. Despite Shabaks' distinct language and recognition as an ethnic group, Kurds wishing to extend land claims into the Nineveh governate claim that Shabaks are really Kurds. The Faili Kurds, who follow Shia Islam, live along the Iran/Iraq border and in Baghdad. Repressed as 'Iranians' under the Saddam regime, they are now targeted for ethnic and religious reasons. In November 2005, two Faili Kurdish mosques in the town of Khanaqin were bombed. The Yezidi are ethnically and linguistically Kurdish but have their own 4,000-year-old religion.

They face persecution by religious extremists as 'devil worshippers'. A Yezidi council member for the Nineveh Plains was assassinated in April 2006, one of 11 Yezidis reported murdered between September 2005 and September 2006.

Iraq is home to many Christian groups, including Chaldo-Assyrians, Syriac-speaking Orthodox Christians, Catholic and Oriental Orthodox Armenians, and Protestants. Chaldo-Assyrians and Syriac Christians both speak the ancient Syriac language and have been in the region since the earliest days of Christianity's spread in the region; they consider themselves Arabs but are not recognized as such by the government. Armenians have been in Mesopotamia since the days of Babylon, their numbers bolstered following the Armenian genocide of 1915. In its September–October human rights report, UNAMI reported increasing violence against all Christians, with a spike in attacks on Christians following the Pope's controversial remarks on Islam in September 2006. Churches and convents were attacked by rocket and gunfire, and a Syriac Orthodox priest was kidnapped and decapitated in October. With mounting violence, many Iraqi churches have cancelled services and the UN reports that Iraqi Christians are fleeing in disproportionate numbers to Syria, Jordan and beyond.

The Mandean-Sabeans are Gnostics who have practised their faith in Iraq for over 2,000 years and speak an endangered language. Their religion forbids the use of violence, which makes them easy targets for Islamic extremists. The state offers no protection from attacks, such as one that killed four Mandean-Sabeans in October 2006. As members of the community flee abroad, the number of Mandean-Sabeans estimated to remain in Iraq in late 2006 was 13,000, down two-thirds since the American-led invasion.

Followers of the Baha'i faith in Iraq are targeted by Islamic extremists because they don't believe Mohammed was the last prophet. For the past 30 years, Baha'i have not been allowed to have citizenship papers or travel documents, which makes it difficult for them to leave the country. Almost entirely gone from Iraq are Jews, who have a 2,600-year history in the country and once numbered 150,000. In October 2005, the UN reported that the only Jews left in Iraq were in Baghdad, and their numbers had shrunk to 20.

Although an estimated 4,000–15,000 Palestinian refugees have left Iraq since 2003, some 20,000 remain and are subject to attack by militias in Baghdad. Favoured as political pawns under Saddam, this mostly Sunni minority now face retaliatory attacks, including by Iraqi security services. Militias have also been seizing Palestinian homes, often for their ethnic kin, who have been displaced by other militias elsewhere in Iraq. The UN received reports of at least six Palestinians killed in June 2006 and the refugee agency reported that many Palestinians were encamped at the Syrian border, trying to flee the country.

Subject to the same sectarian and ethnic targeting as Iraqi men, women face the added burden of gender discrimination. The number of widows in the country is increasing, and Islamic militants leave few opportunities for women to make money, let alone drive or move around without a male relative. The Iraqi government estimates that mixed marriages between Sunni and Shia Arabs account for nearly a third of all marriages in Iraq. In November 2006, the local Peace for Iraqis Association reported that hundreds of Iraqis in mixed sectarian marriages were being forced by militias or their families to divorce, throwing more

women into economic uncertainty. Short-term marriages of convenience, known as Muta'a, were on the rise in 2006; these may serve immediate economic needs of women, but afford them no rights when the marriage is over.

Women across Iraq, many of them non-Muslims, have reported numerous death threats for failing to fully cover their heads and bodies in line with strict Islamic teachings. The Women's Rights Association of Baghdad reported in March 2006 that, since the 2003 invasion, the number of women attacked for failing to cover their heads and faces had more than tripled.

Across Iraq, kidnappings, rapes and sexual slavery of women have increased. UNAMI, in its September–October human rights report, mentions a 'worrying trend of female "suicides" and "attempted suicides" as a result of family conflicts' in the KRG. The government has not aggressively pursued the perpetrators of such 'honour killings', who receive light sentences when they are apprehended and tried. In October, an activist for women's and Arab rights in the Kurdistan region was murdered following threats accusing her of collaboration with international forces. In response to their targeting by militants, many girls' schools did not open this fall.

Although aiming to serve the cause of transitional justice, it appeared that the trial of Saddam Hussein only provided more fodder for sectarian tensions. When Saddam and two co-defendants were sentenced to death on 5 November 2006 for a 1982 massacre of Shia in Dujail, Shia Arabs and Kurds celebrated, while Sunni Arabs saw it as further evidence of their endangerment and loss of privilege. Human Rights Watch criticized the trial's conduct and the verdict's 'suspect' timing, two days before US mid-term Congressional elections. In the course of the trial, three defence attorneys and a witness were assassinated. Although the 'Anfal' trial against Saddam and others for the killing of some 180,000 Kurds was ongoing, Saddam was hanged on 30 December 2006 – the first day of the Muslim holiday Eid-al-Adha as observed by Sunnis.

As Iraqi civil war raged, the report of the Iraq Study Group, commissioned by the US Congress and released in December 2006, stirred enormous controversy in the US and UK but offered few new ideas for Iraq. It was not clear that the weak Iraqi government would be able to establish security for anyone, especially the country's minorities.

Iran

Iran is an ethnically and religiously diverse country whose Shia Persian majority amounts to only slightly more than 50 per cent of the population. In 2006, the Iranian government was embroiled in controversies over its nuclear programme and its backing of Shia militants in neighbouring Iraq, as well as Hezbollah in Lebanon. Receiving less attention was the country's ongoing repression of its many minority groups.

Sunni Arabs make up around 5 per cent of the Iranian population and are concentrated in the south-western, oil-rich province of Khuzistan along the Iraqi border. Over 2006, sectarian civil war in Iraq has led to enhanced calls for Sunni Arab autonomy within Iran, and even independence. Human Rights Watch reported rioting in April 2005 among Sunni Arabs in Khuzistan following a purported letter from a presidential adviser that recommended dispersal of the Arab population. The violence between protesters and police was followed by a series of bombings attributed to Sunni Arab activists in Tehran and Ahwaz in June and October 2005, and January 2006, which killed some 20 people and injured many more. Renewed confrontation between Sunni Arab protesters and Iranian police in March 2006 resulted in three deaths and hundreds of arrests. The Iranian government claims that unrest in Khuzistan is being stirred by British intelligence services across the border.

Kurds, who are mostly Sunni Muslims, make up around 10 per cent of the Iranian population and are concentrated in the north-west, adjacent to the Kurdish populations of Iraq and Turkey. The Iranian government has watched nervously over the course of 2006 as Iraqi Kurds have moved towards greater autonomy, fearing that its Kurds may seek to join an independent Kurdistan. Iranian security forces shot a young Kurd in July 2005, sparking a round of confrontations with the Kurdish minority, and tensions remained palpable through 2006.

Azeris form the largest ethnic minority in Iran at about 25 per cent. These Turkic-speaking Shias live concentrated along the border with Azerbaijan in the north-west of the country and in the capital Tehran. They are relatively well integrated into Iranian society, and Supreme Leader Ayatollah Khamenei is ethnic Azeri. Nonetheless tensions became evident in May 2006 when thousands of Azeris protested in north-west Iran following publication in a government newspaper of a cartoon insulting to Azeris. Government security forces fired on the protesters, killing five and injuring dozens.

The mostly Sunni Baluchi ethnic minority comprises around 2 per cent of the Iranian population, and lives in the impoverished Baluchistan region that straddles the Pakistani border. As Tehran opened a new military base in the area, Baluchi militants attacked a government motorcade in March 2006, killing over 20 people and taking others hostage.

Iran's record on religious freedom continued to be dismal. Baluchis, Kurds and Sunni Arabs decried the fact that not a single Sunni mosque has been permitted in the country, and public displays of Sunni religion remain banned. The 300,000 Baha'i of Iran remain subject to severe state discrimination. In September 2005, state-controlled media began an intense campaign against the Baha'i, whom Islamic clerics decry as heretics for believing that other prophets came after Mohammed. In March 2006, the UN Special Rapporteur on Freedom of Religion said she had received an October 2005 document in which Ayatollah Khamenei ordered the Iranian military to identify and monitor members of the Baha'i community. In May 2006, Human Rights Watch reported the arrests of 54 Baha'i youth volunteers in Shiraz. In February 2006, police and organized gangs broke up a peaceful protest among Nematollahi Sufis (dervishes) in Qom, who complained of a state order to relinquish their place of worship. Hundreds were injured and over a thousand detained. Amnesty International reported that, as of March, at least 173 Sufis remained in detention and that their lawyer had been arrested. The 25,000 Jews of Iran, the largest population in the Middle East outside Israel, continued their coexistence with the Shia Persian majority despite some provocations. In July 2006, during the Lebanon war, an Iranian newspaper falsely reported that Iranian Jews were celebrating Israeli independence day, which prompted extremists to target two synagogues. The community has watched nervously as new Iranian President Mahmoud Ahmadinejad has threatened to 'wipe Israel off the map' and questioned the dimensions of the Holocaust. His campaign promoting Holocaust denial culminated in an international conference held in Tehran in December 2006 – a

move that met with widespread condemnation in Europe and the US.

Women in Iran remained subject to severe restrictions on their rights in accordance with Iran's interpretation of the tenets of *Sharia* law, including the requirement that married women receive their husbands' permission to work. Iran's ruling clerics rejected a suggestion from President Ahmadinejad at

Below: Residents return to find that large areas of southern Beirut had been reduced to rubble by Israeli bombardment during 34 days of conflict between Israel and Hezbollah. Sean Sutton/MAG

the time of the 2006 World Cup that women be allowed to attend football matches, ruling that it was un-Islamic for women to look at strange men's legs. Human Rights Watch reported that, in June 2006, police brutally assaulted hundreds of peaceful protesters in Tehran who were demanding an end to legally sanctioned discrimination against women.

Lebanon

In late 2006, identity politics and sectarian tensions were rising in Lebanon following political assassinations and the fall-out from the July war between Hezbollah and Israel that resulted in over

1,000 civilian deaths, the displacement of over 1 million Lebanese, and the widespread destruction of the country's infrastructure, especially in the south.

Lebanon's Islamic majority is sharply divided into Sunni and Shia groupings that have usually been on opposite sides of political divides, leaving the country without an effective majority. Lebanon's minority groups also display internal political divisions. Lebanon's largest group is Shia Muslims, making up 32 per cent of the population, which has generally felt more drawn to Arab traditions and ties, and thus more open to influence and support from Syria and Iran. Maronite Christians (16 per cent) and Sunni

Muslims (18 per cent) have long dominated Lebanese government and maintained closer relationships with former colonizer France and other Western countries. Smaller minority groups are Palestinians (10 per cent), Druze (7 per cent), Greek Orthodox (5 per cent), Greek Catholic (5 per cent), Armenians (3 per cent), Alawis (3 per cent) and Kurds (1 per cent).

Following its 1975–90 sectarian civil war, Lebanon returned to a modified form of political confessionalism, whereby government positions are apportioned among the main religious groups of the country. This system has led to under-representation of smaller minorities in government, with the Druze community in particular chafing at its limitations.

Palestinian refugees have been particularly marginalized in Lebanon. About half of the country's 400,000 Palestinians live in the south and half of them live in camps. Palestinians are denied citizenship and, although restrictions were loosened in June 2005, they remain barred from many professions and relegated to manual labour.

The country's ethnic and religious groups live largely segregated throughout the country. Shia, concentrated in the south, felt neglected by successive Maronite–Sunni governments in Beirut, and formed Hezbollah with Iranian and Syrian backing in response to the 1982 Israeli invasion of Lebanon. Following the February 2005 assassination of the Sunni former Lebanese Prime Minister Rafiq al-Hariri, Sunni, Christian and Druze opponents of broad Syrian influence in Lebanon took to the streets to launch the March 2005 'Cedar Revolution', while Hezbollah and the Shia community demonstrated in support of Syria. Hezbollah complained bitterly when anti-Syrian forces won control of parliament two months later and, with the support of the UN Security Council, prodded Syria to end its 30-year military occupation.

In July 2006, Hezbollah abducted two Israeli soldiers along the border, sparking a fierce Israeli military assault on Lebanon. While the brunt of the attack came in the Hezbollah stronghold in southern Lebanon, from where the organization had long fired rockets indiscriminately into northern Israel, it extended to most parts of Lebanon. Lebanon was cut off from the outside world through a naval blockade and the bombing of runways at Beirut airport and strategic road infrastructure throughout the country, ostensibly to prevent Hezbollah's re-supply from Syria. The

bombings, and an Israeli ground invasion, continued until 14 August, as did Hezbollah rocket fire into Israel. Human rights organizations blamed both sides for the indiscriminate nature of their attacks, which killed over 1,000 Lebanese and 43 Israeli civilians. The United Nations estimated that, as of 1 November 2006, 150,000–200,000 Lebanese remained displaced as a result of the conflict.

The already vulnerable Palestinian refugee community in southern Lebanon was particularly hard hit by the war. Not only were some of their camps and homes damaged or destroyed by Israeli air raids, but many lost their livelihoods. Israel made broad use of cluster bombs during the war, and hundreds of thousands of unexploded munitions now litter southern Lebanese agricultural fields on which many Palestinian labourers depend for their income.

In September 2006, Refugees International warned that displaced Christians and Sunni Muslims in the majority Shia south were reluctant to return home for fear of discrimination by Hezbollah. Indeed, Hezbollah appeared to be more effective than the government in providing cash assistance to those residents of the south whose homes had been destroyed in the bombing.

During the war, as Israel targeted all parts of Lebanon, destroying its booming tourist season and setting back its economic development by years, many Lebanese of all communities rallied around Hezbollah in their anger. However, shortly after the war, representatives of non-Shia communities were loud in their remonstrations against Hezbollah for having provoked Israel and having brought such destruction to Lebanon.

On 11 November 2006, all Shia members of government resigned, ending its ethnic balance. Subsequent parliamentary approval of an international investigation into the Hariri assassination fuelled Hezbollah demands that the government step down to pave the way for new elections that the organization felt should end Shia under-representation.

The assassination of Industry Minister and Maronite Christian leader Pierre Gemayel on 21 November 2006 resulted in the further sharpening of sectarian tensions. Many Sunni, Druze and Christians, and, internationally, the United States, immediately suspected Syrian involvement, and the UN Security Council approved the establishment of an international criminal tribunal to investigate the

Hariri and Gemayel assassinations, as well as other killings of prominent anti-Syrian figures since early 2005. Political leaders and Lebanese citizens alike appeared to be balancing their anger and sense of injustice with wariness about nearing the abyss of war.

Israel

Israel continued to be pulled between its foundation as a 'Jewish state' and its claim to full democracy, inherent to which is respect for the rights of Palestinian Arabs who comprise 20 per cent of the Israeli population. Around 85 per cent of these are Muslim, and they are the fastest growing community in Israel, which many Jews regard as a threat to the Jewish identity of Israel. Continued attacks on Israel from the occupied territories of the West Bank and Gaza Strip have further complicated efforts to secure the rights of this minority.

In 2006, race continued to form the basis for many Israeli government actions. In 2003, Israeli legislators instituted race-based discrimination against Palestinian Arab citizens seeking to acquire citizenship for spouses in the occupied territories, forcing thousands of families to separate. In May 2006, the Israeli Supreme Court narrowly rejected a challenge to the law. Bedouins, who make up an estimated 8.5 per cent of the Israeli Palestinian population, faced continued Israeli government efforts to change the demographics in southern Israel through the support of Jewish settlements and neglect of services to and demolition of Arab Bedouin homes in the Naqab (Negev) desert region. In August and September 2006, courts issued orders for the destruction of 12 Bedouin homes in 'unrecognized' villages. Following the July 2006 war with Hezbollah in Lebanon, the Israeli Finance Minister issued an order for compensation for Israeli border towns that suffered during the war, but systematically excluded Arab communities from the scheme. In November 2006, a draft action plan to close the gap between Jewish and Arab Israelis in educational resources had the broad agreement of Israel's Union of Local Authorities and the Higher Arab Monitoring Committee, but had received only a tepid response from the Israeli Education Ministry, which wanted to spread the resources for the project over a longer time-frame. Arab Druze, the only ethnic minority subject to military conscription, make up around 1.5 per cent of the Israeli population, and have chafed at military service out of opposition to Israeli policy in the occupied territories. The Arab Druze Initiative, an organization of conscientious objectors to military service, estimated in April 2006 that the number of Druze youth refusing military service had climbed to 40 per cent, despite the threat of arrest.

Palestine

The Israeli-occupied territories of the West Bank (including East Jerusalem) and Gaza are home to 2.3 million indigenous Palestinians and 280,000 Jewish settlers. To the extent that Israel continues to exercise authority over the territories, it assumes much responsibility under international law for public order and safety, the rule of law and the rights of the population.

The election of a Hamas-led government in January 2006 by Palestinians fed up with the long-ruling Fatah Party's corruption and its inability to move the political process forward led Western countries to impose strict economic sanctions on the Palestinian Authority in an attempt to bring about its recognition of Israel, acceptance of past peace agreements and renunciation of violence. Meanwhile, violence between Hamas and Fatah factions escalated during 2006, especially in Gaza, as both adjusted to their new roles in government and opposition, respectively.

Following the abduction of an Israeli soldier by Palestinian militants and repeated and indiscriminate firing of home-made missiles from the occupied territories into Israel, Israel launched a new military incursion into Gaza on 25 June 2006. Israeli forces bombed Gaza's only independent power station, cutting 43 per cent of the territory's electricity supply. According to an Israeli human rights organization, B'Tselem, through October 2006, over 375 Palestinians had been killed in the sustained assault, including 199 civilians. A tenuous ceasefire in November 2006 provided some hope that negotiations might soon begin.

In the West Bank, the separation barrier that Israel began building in 2002 with the stated intent to enhance its defences against terrorist attacks had reached a length of 670 km by late 2006. The wall carves off 10 per cent of the West Bank to the Israeli side, including settlements on Palestinian land, and in July 2004 the International Court of Justice found that it gravely infringed Palestinian rights. 200,000 Palestinians caught on the western side of the wall are effectively imprisoned between the hours of 10 pm and 6 am, denied entry if they miss the curfew, and denied access to emergency services during these hours. UN High Commissioner for Human Rights Louise Arbour remarked, in November 2006, 'Here you have one people balancing their right to security against another people's right to freedom.' Palestinian freedom of movement between the West Bank and Gaza, as well as the passage of goods at Karni crossing, also remained curtailed, with drastic economic consequences.

In July 2005 Israeli law-makers barred Palestinians in the occupied territories from seeking compensation for deaths, injury or damages caused by Israeli security forces since the beginning of the Second Intifada in September 2000. Israeli and Palestinian human rights organizations filed a challenge to the law before the Israeli Supreme Court in September 2005. The Court rejected part of the law in December 2006, ruling that Palestinians could seek redress for damages stemming from non-combat military operations.

Just under 2 per cent of indigenous Palestinians in the occupied territories are Christian, and these reside largely in Bethlehem, Jerusalem and Ramallah. Following the Pope's controversial remarks on Islam in September 2006, seven churches in the Palestinian territories were set on fire. While Hamas leader and Palestinian Authority Prime Minister Ismail Haniya condemned the Pope's statement, he also denounced the attacks on Christian churches in the occupied territories.

Syria

Sectarian tension in Syria is rising as the majority Sunni Arab country grows alarmed at the fate of the Sunni minority in Iraq, and increasingly sympathetic to such Sunni militant organizations as al-Qaeda, who purport to defend Sunnis and bring retribution to Shia. Iraqi refugees, including Shia, have streamed into Syria, and in June 2006 sectarian rioting erupted in a largely Iraqi Damascus suburb.

There are an estimated 1.5 million Kurds in Syria, although an estimated 300,000 remain stateless following a 1962 decision that stripped many Kurds and their descendants of their citizenship, and the presence of many more without official papers. Police violently prevented an October 2006 rally in Damascus in support of these stateless Kurds, who are barred from property ownership, admission to university and public sector employment. Amnesty International raised alarm over the arrest in

November 2006 of a Syrian Kurdish activist who had been demanding an investigation into the May 2005 torture and murder of his father – allegedly by Syrian Military Intelligence officers.

Saudi Arabia

During 2006, Saudi Arabia remained an abyss in the area of religious freedom. The absolute monarchy, though itself the target of al-Qaeda attacks in recent years, continued to foster Sunni extremism directed toward the West, religious minorities and women.

Despite some recent efforts at their revision, educational materials used in Saudi schools still fan religious intolerance toward Jews, Shia Muslims and Christians. The US Commission on International Religious Freedom reported that, in 2006, clerics authorized by the Ministry of Islamic Affairs continued to engage in hate speech. In April 2006, the government arrested a Saudi journalist for criticism of the government's strict interpretation of Islam.

Since the founding of the Kingdom of Saudi Arabia, the country's minority Shia – comprising around 10 per cent of the population – have faced restrictions on religious practice and discrimination in education, employment and representation in government. King Abdullah formally took power in August 2005 and has taken some steps to ease tension with the Shia minority by releasing political prisoners and allowing greater political participation by Shia. Nevertheless, the International Crisis Group reported in September 2005 that the sectarian war in Iraq had worsened relations between Sunnis and Shia in Saudi Arabia.

The 700,000 Ismaili Muslims in Saudi Arabia likewise have faced rampant discrimination, as the government has closed their mosques and accused them of blasphemy, apostasy and witchcraft. In November 2006, King Abdullah pardoned a group of Ismailis jailed after rioting in 2000, but the Saudi-based Human Rights First Society reported that at least two other Ismailis remained imprisoned for insulting the Prophet Mohammed. It was not clear whether this included Hadi al Mutif, an Ismaili sentenced to death in 1996 for allegedly committing that offence in 1993.

Kuwait

Pressure on the government from the National Assembly may improve the situation of 'Bidouns' (meaning 'without' in Arabic) in Kuwait, who number 100,000–120,000, or around 5 per cent of the population. Bidouns are Arabs who have long been resident in Kuwait but are denied citizenship rights as the Kuwaiti government maintains they are really Saudi or other nationals who seek citizenship to take advantage of generous Kuwaiti social benefits. Despite some improvements in 2005, notably provision of health care to the children of Bidouns, this minority still faces discrimination in employment, freedom of movement and education. In November 2006, a number of MPs attended a Bidoun rights forum hosted by the Kuwaiti Human Rights Society, where they urged the government to grant greater citizenship rights to Bidouns and indicated that formal parliamentary hearings on the issue were in the offing. The MPs were particularly concerned that Bidouns who have served in the Kuwaiti military, and the families of Bidoun soldiers who have died for Kuwait, are still denied basic rights of citizenship.

Gulf States: migrant workers

The oil-producing Gulf States rely heavily for labour on migrant workers, mostly from South and South-East Asia, as well as other Arab countries. Lax or non-existent labour laws have led to widespread exploitative work conditions and restricted freedom of movement for migrants, which led to unheard-of strikes in the oil industry. Women migrant workers are especially subject to physical and sexual violence. Human Rights Watch released a report in November 2006 detailing the reliance on exploitative labour of 600,000 Asian migrants to fuel the building boom in the United Arab Emirates (UAE). On the eve of the report's release, the UAE announced sweeping labour reforms. There were also some moves toward reform in Saudi Arabia, where migrant workers make up around 33 per cent of the population; King Abdullah signed a new labour law in September 2005 that entitles migrant workers to one day off per week, and 21 days for holidays per year. Oman and Bahrain enacted legislation in 2006 to legalize labour unions.

Many migrant workers arrive in the region through human traffickers and are surprised to find themselves in exploitative situations. In November 2006, a Special Rapporteur on trafficking for the UN Human Rights Council travelled through the Gulf States. She criticized Oman and Qatar for treating trafficked migrant workers as criminals rather than victims, and noted a pending anti-trafficking bill in Bahrain, as well as its establishment of safe houses for abused migrant workers. ▪

Reference
Compiled by Marusca Perazzi

Notes to Table 1

Sources of the indicators are as follows:

- *Conflict indicators*: The base data used was Marshall/Gurr/Khosla, Center for International Development and Conflict Management, University of Maryland, updated for 2006 using latest figures from Marshall, Center for Systemic Peace, and Heidelberg Institute for International Conflict Research.
  Self-determinations conflicts in 2006 were ranked on a scale of 0–5 as follows: 5=ongoing armed conflict; 4=contained armed conflict; 3=settled armed conflict; 2=militant politics; 1=conventional politics. Major armed conflicts were classified as 2=ongoing in late 2006; 1=emerging from conflict since 2001.
- *Prior genocide or politicide*: Harff, US Political Instability Task Force (formerly State Failure Task Force). 1=one or more episodes since 1945.
- *Indicators of group division*: Failed States Index, Fund for Peace and the Carnegie Endowment for International Peace, 2006.
- *Democracy/governance indicators*: Annual Good Governance Indicators, World Bank, 2006.
- *OECD country risk classification*: Organisation for Economic Cooperation and Development, country risk classification prevailing at October 2006. Where no classification is given, a value of 8 was accorded.

Full bibliographic references are given in the Select Bibliography.

Indicators were rebased as necessary to give an equal weighting to the five categories above, with the exception of the prior geno-/politicide indicator. As a dichotomous variable this received a lesser weighting to avoid too great a distortion to the final ranking. Resulting values were then summed.

The full formula is:

$$(A/2) + (Bx1.25) + (Cx2) + (D+E+F)/6 + (G+H+I)/-1 + (Jx0.625)$$

Note that Djibouti is ranked artificially low due to the absence of data on some of the indicators. Israel/Occupied Territories/Palestinian Authority is also ranked artificially low as some of the indicators only apply to the state of Israel and not to the Occupied Territories.

The methodology for the choice of indicators was described in *State of the World's Minorities 2006*. It is based on compiling current data to approximate the main known antecedents of genocide or political mass killing, drawing on the work of Barbara Harff and others. Responsibility for the table and any errors or omissions remains with Minority Rights Group International.

Country	Group	A. Self-determination conflicts	B. Major armed conflict	C. Prior genocide/politicide
		Conflict indicators		

Table 1
Peoples under threat 2007

Country	Group	A. Self-determination conflicts	B. Major armed conflict	C. Prior genocide/politicide
Somalia	Darood, Hawiye, Issaq and other clans; Bantu and other groups	4	2	1
Iraq	Shia, Sunni, Kurds, Turkomans, Christians, Smaller minorites	4	2	1
Sudan	Fur, Zaghawa, Massalit and others in Darfur; Dinka, Nuer and others in the South; Nuba, Beja	5	2	1
Afghanistan	Hazara, Pashtun, Tajiks, Uzbeks	4	2	1
Burma	Kachin, Karenni, Karen, Mons, Rohingyas, Shan, Chin (Zomis), Wa	5	2	1
Dem. Rep. of the Congo	Hema and Lendu, Hunde, Hutu, Luba, Lunda, Tutsi/Banyamulenge, Twa/Mbuti	1	2	1
Nigeria	Ibo, Ijaw, Ogoni, Yoruba, Hausa (Muslims) and Christians in the North	5	2	1
Pakistan	Ahmadiyya, Baluchis, Hindus, Mohhajirs, Pashtun, Sindhis	5	2	1
Angola	Bakongo, Cabindans, Ovimbundu	4	1	1
Russian Federation	Chechens, Ingush, Lezgins, indigenous northern peoples, Roma	5	2	1
Burundi	Hutu, Tutsi, Twa	0	1	1
Uganda	Acholi, Karamojong	1	2	1
Ethiopia	Anuak, Afars, Oromo, Somalis	5	0	1
Sri Lanka	Tamils, Muslims	5	2	1
Haiti	Political/social targets	0	2	0
Côte d'Ivoire	Northern Mande (Dioula), Senoufo, Bete, newly-settled groups	0	1	0
Rwanda	Hutu, Tutsi, Twa	0	1	1
Nepal	Political/social targets, Dalits	0	2	0
Philippines	Indigenous peoples, Moros (Muslims)	5	2	1
Iran	Arabs, Azeris, Baha'is, Baluchis, Kurds, Turkomans	5	0	1
Indonesia	Acehnese, Chinese, Dayaks, Madurese, Papuans	4	1	1
Bosnia and Herzegovina	Croats, Bosniac Muslims, Serbs	4	0	1
Serbia	Ethnic Albanians, Croats, Roma, Ashkali, Serbs (Kosovo)	4	0	1
Chad	Southerners	3	0	0
Zimbabwe	Ndebele, Europeans	1	0	0
Liberia	Dan, Krahn, Ma, other groups	0	1	0
Colombia	Political/social targets, Afro-descendants, indigenous peoples	3	2	0
Uzbekistan	Tajiks, Islamic political groups, Russians	1	0	0
Syria	Kurds	0	0	1

Reference

State of the World's
Minorities 2007

D. Massive movement – refugees and IDPs	E. Legacy of vengeance – group grievance	F. Rise of factionalized elites	G. Voice and accountability	H. Political stability	I. Rule of law	J. OECD country risk classification	
8.1	8	9.8	-1.89	-2.51	-2.36	7	21.95
8.3	9.8	9.7	-1.47	-2.82	-1.81	7	21.61
9.7	9.7	9.1	-1.84	-2.05	-1.48	7	21.50
9.6	9.1	8	-1.28	-2.12	-1.68	8	21.03
8.8	9	8	-2.16	-1	-1.56	7	20.40
9.5	9.1	9.6	-1.64	-2.4	-1.76	7	19.88
5.9	9.1	9	-0.69	-1.77	-1.38	7	19.22
9.3	8.6	9.1	-1.23	-1.68	-0.81	6	18.97
8.5	6.3	8	-1.15	-0.82	-1.28	7	16.68
7.2	8	9	-0.85	-1.07	-0.84	4	16.29
9.1	7	7.8	-1.15	-1.65	-1.17	8	16.20
9.2	7.8	7.9	-0.59	-1.32	-0.74	7	16.18
7.6	7	8.7	-1.1	-1.48	-0.77	7	16.11
8.2	9.1	8.9	-0.26	-1.25	0	5	16.00
5	8.8	9.6	-1.41	-1.91	-1.62	7	15.72
7.6	9.8	9.8	-1.5	-2.49	-1.47	7	15.62
7	9	8.9	-1.32	-1.21	-1	7	15.31
4.8	9.2	9	-1.19	-2.36	-0.81	7	15.07
5.5	7.2	7.2	0.01	-1.11	-0.52	5	15.06
8.7	6.9	8.8	-1.43	-1.14	-0.76	5	15.02
8.2	6.3	7.9	-0.21	-1.42	-0.87	5	14.61
8.5	8.6	8.7	-0.11	-0.78	-0.74	7	14.31
8.5	8.6	8.6	0.12	-0.91	-0.81	7	14.26
9	8.5	9.5	-1.25	-1.34	-1.23	7	14.20
8.9	8.5	8.5	-1.65	-1.58	-1.47	7	13.89
9.3	7	8.8	-0.92	-1.45	-1.6	7	13.78
9.1	7.4	9.2	-0.32	-1.79	-0.71	4	13.60
5.8	7.5	9.1	-1.76	-1.91	-1.31	7	13.59
7.1	8	7.1	-1.67	-0.91	-0.42	7	13.08

Country	Group	A. Self-determination conflicts	B. Major armed conflict	C. Prior genocide/politicide

Table 1 (continued)
Peoples under threat 2007

Country	Group	A. Self-determination conflicts	B. Major armed conflict	C. Prior genocide/politicide
Cambodia	Cham, Vietnamese	0	0	1
Equatorial Guinea	Bubi	2	0	1
Laos	Hmong	4	0	0
Yemen	Political/social targets	0	1	0
Bangladesh	Ahmadiyya, Hindus, other religious minorities, Chittagong Hill Tribes	3	0	0
Lebanon	Druze, Maronite Christians, Palestinians, Shia, Sunnis	2	1	0
Algeria	Berbers	2	1	1
Azerbaijan	Armenians	4	0	0
Central African Republic	Political/social targets, Aka	0	0	0
Turkey	Kurds, Roma	5	2	0
Guinea	Fulani, Malinke	0	0	0
Georgia	Adzhars, Abkhazians, South Ossetians	4	0	0
Kyrgyzstan	Uzbeks, Russians	1	0	0
Eritrea	Afars	0	0	0
Tajikistan	Uzbeks, Russians	0	0	0
Cameroon	Westerners	2	0	0
Sierra Leone	All groups incl. Krio, Limba, Mende, Temne	0	1	0
North Korea	Political/social targets, religious minorities	0	0	0
Moldova	Trans-Dniester Slavs	4	0	0
Togo	Ewe, Kabre	0	0	0
China	Tibetans, Uyghurs, Hui, religious minorities	4	0	1
Turkmenistan	Political/social targets, Russians	0	0	0
Vietnam	Montagnards	2	0	1
Thailand	Chinese, Malay-Muslims, Northern Hill Tribes	5	2	0
Israel/OT/PA	Palestinians in Gaza/West Bank, Israeli Palestinians	5	2	0
Bolivia	Indigenous Highland, Indigenous Lowland	2	0	0
Guatemala	Indigenous peoples	0	0	1
Niger	Djerema-songhai, Hausa, Tuaregs	3	0	0
Cuba	Political/social targets	0	0	0
Ecuador	Afro-descendants, indigenous peoples	2	0	0
Belarus	Poles	0	0	0
Nicaragua	Indigenous peoples, Creoles	3	0	0
India	Assamese, Bodos, Nagas, Tripuras, other Adivasis, Kashmiris, Sikhs, Muslims, Dalits	5	2	0

Indicators of group division			Democracy/governance indicators				Total
D. Massive movement – refugees and IDPs	E. Legacy of vengeance – group grievance	F. Rise of factionalized elites	G. Voice and accountability	H. Political stability	I. Rule of law	J. OECD country risk classification	
6.5	7	7.5	-0.94	-0.44	-1.13	8	13.01
2	6.7	8	-1.71	0.21	-1.33	7	12.99
5.9	6.3	8.9	-1.54	-0.27	-1.12	7	12.82
6.7	7	9.4	-1.07	-1.61	-1.1	6	12.63
5.8	9.5	8.9	-0.5	-1.65	-0.87	6	12.30
4.3	7.8	8.3	-0.72	-1.14	-0.36	7	12.25
6.6	7.1	6.4	-0.92	-1.09	-0.71	3	12.20
8.1	7.3	7.5	-1.16	-1.21	-0.84	5	12.15
7.7	8.8	8	-1.15	-1.13	-1.29	7	12.03
6.1	7.3	6.9	-0.04	-0.54	0.07	5	12.02
7.2	8.1	9	-1.18	-1.11	-1.11	7	11.83
6.8	7.4	7.1	-0.27	-0.8	-0.82	7	11.82
6.6	7	7.9	-1.03	-1.21	-1.07	7	11.77
7.2	5.4	7.5	-1.83	-0.72	-0.81	8	11.71
6.6	6.2	8.7	-1.17	-1.35	-0.99	7	11.47
6.8	6.5	7.9	-1.19	-0.34	-1.02	7	11.46
7.9	7.1	7.7	-0.38	-0.48	-1.12	7	11.39
6	7.2	8	-2.06	-0.12	-1.15	7	11.24
4.7	7.3	6.8	-0.49	-0.65	-0.59	7	11.24
5.8	6	7.8	-1.23	-1.22	-1.07	7	11.16
5.1	8	8	-1.66	-0.18	-0.47	2	11.08
4.2	5.2	8	-1.95	-0.34	-1.41	7	10.98
6.5	5.3	7	-1.6	0.34	-0.45	5	10.97
5.7	8.1	7.2	0.07	-0.55	-0.1	3	10.96
8.5	9	7.5	0.61	-1.16	0.76	3	10.83
4	7	8.4	-0.09	-1.15	-0.78	7	10.63
6	7.1	6	-0.37	-0.89	-1.04	5	10.61
4.3	8.5	6	-0.06	-0.56	-0.82	7	10.45
4.7	5.5	8	-1.87	0.03	-1.14	7	10.39
4.8	6.8	7.3	-0.16	-0.83	-0.84	7	10.36
5.1	5.5	8	-1.68	0.01	-1.04	7	10.19
5.5	6.4	7	0.01	-0.16	-0.7	7	9.88
2.8	6.9	5.7	0.35	-0.85	0.09	3	9.85

Country	Group	A. Self-determination conflicts	B. Major armed conflict	C. Prior genocide/politicide

Table 1 (continued)
Peoples under threat 2007

Country	Group	A. Self-determination conflicts	B. Major armed conflict	C. Prior genocide/politicide
Venezuela	Indigenous peoples, Afro-descendants	0	0	0
Macedonia	Albanians, Roma, Serbs	3	0	0
Kenya	Borana, Endorois, Kalenjin, Maasai, Ogiek, Somalis, Turkana	0	0	0
Bhutan	Lhotshampa, Nepalese	2	0	0
Mauritania	Black Moors, Kewri	0	0	0
Papua New Guinea	Bounganvilleans	3	0	0
Ukraine	Tatars, Russians (Crimea)	2	0	0
Djibouti	Afars	3	0	0

Indicators of group division			Democracy/governance indicators				Total
D. Massive movement – refugees and IDPs	E. Legacy of vengeance – group grievance	F. Rise of factionalized elites	G. Voice and accountability	H. Political stability	I. Rule of law	J. OECD country risk classification	
4.8	6.8	7.3	-0.5	-1.22	-1.22	6	9.84
5.1	7.1	6.2	-0.03	-1.04	-0.38	6	9.77
7.1	6.7	7.6	-0.12	-1.16	-0.94	6	9.54
8.1	7	8.4	-1.05	1.01	0.52	8	9.44
5.9	8.5	7.9	-1.09	0.31	-0.54	7	9.41
2.5	8	6.7	-0.05	-0.81	-0.92	5	9.27
3.8	7.2	7.5	-0.26	-0.39	-0.6	6	9.08
			-0.84	-0.74	-0.87	8	8.95

Table 2
Minority members in national legislatures

Rank	Country	Minority	Seat %	Minority population %	Under/over	LSQ Score	Number of elections
1	South Africa**	White	29.3	14.0	(15.3)	3.22	2
		Coloured	8.9	8.0	(0.9)		2
		Indian	6.9	2.4	(4.5)		2
2	Namibia	White	9.0	5.0	(4.0)	2.84	1
		Kavango	6.4	8.0	(-1.6)		
		Damara	7.7	6.6	(1.1)		
		Herero	12.8	6.0	(6.8)		
		Nama	6.4	4.0	(2.4)		
		Coloured	3.8	3.0	(0.8)		
		Caprivian	5.1	3.0	(2.1)		
		San	1.3	2.0	(-0.7)		
		Baster	3.8	2.0	(1.8)		
		Tswana	0	0.6	(-0.6)		
3	Tanzania	Zanzibaris	18.6	2.8	(15.8)	2.81	1
4	Belgium*	Francoph.	40.3	32.0	(8.3)	2.04	4
5	Bosnia-H	Bosniac	33.3	43.7	(-10.4)	1.94	1
			33.3	17.3	(16.0)		
			33.3	31.4	(-1.9)		
6	Fr. Polynesia	Whites	15.8	10.1	(5.7)	1.91	1
		Chinese	5.3	3.7	(1.6)		
7	Lebanon	Shia	21.1	32.0	(-10.9)	1.88	1
		Sunni	21.1	18.0	(3.1)		
		Maronites	26.6	16.0	(10.6)		
		Druze	4.7	7.0	(-2.3)		
		Greek Orth.	10.9	5.0	(5.9)		
		Greek Cath.	6.2	5.0	(1.2)		
		Armenians	3.9	3.0	(0.9)		
		Alawis	1.6	3.0	(-1.4)		
8	Netherlands	AF/ME/Turk	6.7	4.0	(2.7)	1.53	1
		Caribbean	3.3	1.3	(2.0)		
9	Canada	Francoph.*	24.5	20.9	(3.6)	1.41	3
		Asians	5.2	1.5	(3.7)		
		Black	1.3	1.2	(0.1)		
		Inuit	0.6	3.5	(2.9)		
10	Switzerland	Francoph.	24.0	21.0	(3.0)	1.34	1
		Italophones	4.0	4.3	(-0.3)		1
		Romansh	1.5	0.6	(0.9)		1
11	New Zealand	Maori	16.0	12.3	(3.7)	1.30	1
		Pacific Islanders	3.0	5.0	(-2.0)		
		Asian	2.0	0.5	(1.5)		
12	Slovenia*	Hungarians	1.1	0.4	(0.7)	1.20	4
		Italians	2.3	0.1	(2.2)		4
13	Sri Lanka	Tamils	16.9	18.0	(-1.1)	1.0	1
		Muslims	10.7	7.6	(3.1)		
14	Finland*	Swedes	7.7	5.8	(1.9)	0.97	3
15	Kiribati	Banabans	2.4	0.6	(1.8)	0.95	1
16	Sweden	Med/Mid East	1.8	1.9	(-0.1)	0.89	1
		Black	1.2	0.1	(1.1)		
		Latino	0.6	0.1	(0.5)		
		Sami	0.3	0.2	(0.1)		
17	Slovakia*	Hungarians	12.4	10.8	(1.6)	0.81	5
		Russians	0.7	1.0	(-0.3)		5
18	Zambia	White	0.7	0.1	(0.6)	0.77	1
		Asian	0.7	0.1	(0.6)		
19	Malawi	Asian	1.0	0.1	(0.9)	0.67	1

Rank	Country	Minority	Seat %	Minority population %	Under/over	LSQ Score	Number of elections
20	**Iraq**	Kurds	23.4	22.0	(1.4)	**0.55**	1
		Sunni	23.4	17.0	(6.4)		
		Turkmen	0.4	4.0	(-3.6)		
		Christian	0.4	4.0	(-3.6)		
21	**Albania**	Greeks	3.6	3.1	(0.5)	**0.5**	1
22	**Zimbabwe**	White	0.7	0.5	(0.2)	**0.32**	1
23	**Dennmark**	Muslim	1.1	1.3	(-0.2)	**0.3**	1
		Inuit	1.1	0.9	(0.2)		
		Faroese	1.1	0.9	(0.2)		
24	**Papua New Guinea**	Bougainvilleans	3.7	4.0	(-0.3)	**-0.39**	1
25	**Ireland**	Non-Whites	0.0	0.5	(-0.5)	**-0.5**	1
26	**Australia***	Aborigines	0.0	1.4	(-1.4)	**-0.84**	5
27	**Norway**	Asian	0.6	2.0	(-1.4)	**-0.84**	1
28	**Mongolia**	Kazaks	4.2	5.9	(-1.7)	**-0.92**	2
29	**Poland**	Germans	0.4	2.4	(-2.0)	**-1.0**	1
30	**Pakistan**	Non-Muslims	2.9	5.0	(-2.1)	**-1.02**	1
31	**Germany**	Nth. Af/Mid East	0.6	3.0	(-2.4)	**-1.09**	1
32	**Bulgaria***	Turks	6.9	9.4	(-2.5)	**-1.1**	4
33	**UK**	Afro-Caribbean	0.6	0.9	(-0.3)	**-1.12**	3
		Asian	0.7	2.9	(-2.2)		3
34	**Trinidad & Tobago**	Afro	41.7	37.0	(4.7)	**-1.26**	1
		Mixed	11.1	20.0	(-8.9)		
		Chinese	3.0	2.0	(1.0)		
35	**Azerbaijan**	Lezgins	0.8	4.0	(-3.2)	**-1.27**	1
36	**Fiji**	Indo-Fijian	38.0	42.0	(-4.0)	**-1.41**	1
37	**Romania***	Hungarians	7.5	7.1	(-0.4)	**-1.41**	3
		Roma	0.3	1.8	(-1.5)		3
38	**France**	Nth Africa	0.2	2.5	(-2.3)	**-1.64**	1
		Overseas territ.	0.7	3.8	(-3.1)		
39	**India***	Muslims	5.3	11.4	(-6.1)	**-1.92**	4
		Dalits	14.5	15.8	(-1.3)		
		Adivasis	7.5	7.5	(0.0)		
40	**United States***	African Amer.	8.4	12.1	(-3.7)	**-2.12**	7
		Latino	4.3	8.9	(-4.6)		7
		Native Amer.	0.1	0.8	(-0.7)		7
41	**Lithuania***	Poles	3.1	7.0	(-3.9)	**-2.24**	3
		Russians	2.4	8.5	(-6.1)		3
42	**Israel**	Arabs	7.5	17.5	(-10.0)	**-2.29**	4
		Druze	1.0	1.5	(-0.5)		4
43	**Croatia**	Serbs	2.4	12.2	(-9.8)	**-2.56**	1
		Czech	0.8	0.7	(-0.1)		
		Hungarian	0.8	0.5	(-0.3)		
		Italian	0.8	0.4	(-0.4)		
		Others	1.6	5.7	(-4.1)		
44	**Macedonia**	Albanians	23.0	23.0	(-12.2)	**-2.93**	1
		Turks	4.0	4.0	(-2.3)		
		Roma	2.3	2.3	(-1.5)		
		Serbs	2.0	2.0	(-1.2)		

Table 2 (continued)
Minority members in national legislatures

Rank	Country	Minority	Seat %	Minority population %	Under/over	LSQ Score	Number of elections
45	**Afghanistan**	Hazara	12.0	16.0	(-4.0)	**-3.22**	1
		Tajik	21.3	30.0	(-8.7)		
		Uzbek	8.0	13.0	(-5.0)		
		Kuchi	4.0	7.0	(-3.0)		
46	**Brazil**	Afro	3.9	13.2	(-9.3)	**-3.28**	1
47	**Spain**	Catalan	5.1	16.0	(-10.9)	**-3.29**	1
		Galician	0.6	7.9	(-7.3)		
		Basque	2.3	2.0	(-0.3)		
		Canary Is.	0.9	4.6	(-3.7)		
48	**Latvia***	Russians	9.3	33.1	(-23.8)	**-3.45**	4
49	**Estonia***	Russophones	4.7	30.3	(-25.6)	**-3.58**	4
50	**Montenegro**	Albanians	2.6	5.0	(-2.4)	**-3.65**	1
		Serbians	7.8	32.0	(-24.2)		

Key: Minority percentage: MRG, *World Directory of Minorities* (London: MRG 1997).
Seat percentages are from the most recent election unless noted.
Data is for the lower house in bicameral parliaments, current to 1 December 2006 unless otherwise stated.
* 1990–2003 average data from Lublin 2006.
**South Africa 1994 and 1999.

Sources: Data collected by Andrew Reynolds, Marusca Perazzi from MRG and partners of MRG. Very grateful thanks go to Catherine Kannam, Susan Glover, Wendy Wolford, Altin Iranjani, Bernt Aardal, Krzysztof Jasiewicz, Michael Gallagher, Burt Monroe, John Carey, Nenad Stojanovic, Juan Díez-Nicolás and the Center for Peace, Legal Advice and Psychosocial Assistance, Vukovar, Croatia.

See also: Stojanovic, N. (2006) 'Do multicultural democracies really require PR? Counterevidence from Switzerland', *Swiss Political Science Review* 12(4), forthcoming; Lublin, D. (2006), forthcoming.

Adapted LSQ Index
The Least Squares Index used to aggregate minority under/over-representation in this table was invented by Michael Gallagher of Trinity College Dublin to measure electoral system disproportionality. In principle it treats one group with 15 percent of the population but no seats as a *more* disproportional outcome than 15 groups each winning 1 per cent less of the seats than their population share would suggest. Thus the measure gives a more accurate impression of minority inclusion.

P_i = population share for group i
S_i = seat share for group i
Index = $\sqrt{.5 \cdot \text{sum of all } (P_i - S_i) \text{ squared}}$

The adaptation of Gallagher's LSQ Index used in this table is that positives and negatives of each disproportionality have remained in the equation.

A note on data gathering
This report represents the first time that data on minority MPs in national parliaments has been systematically collected across a large number of countries and continents. We have sought to be as accurate as possible and focus on self-identified minority MPs. We have relied upon in-country expertise wherever possible. Our minority categorizations and population shares come from MRG's *Directory of World Minorities* (1997). There will be some disputes about population size and what constitutes a minority group. There may be questions about whether an MP really is from a minority group and issues of basic counting error. In future iterations of this survey we hope to include many more national legislatures.

Reference

Table 3
Explaining minority representation

Rep. rank	Country	Electoral system	HDI ranking	Dem. score	Reserv. seats?	Region
1	South Africa	List PR	121	3	No	AFR
2	Namibia	List PR	125	4	No	AFR
3	Tanzania	FPTP	162	7	Yes	AFR
4	Belgium	List PR	13	2	No	WEUR
5	Bosnia-H	List PR	62	7	Yes	CEEUR
6	Fr. Polynesia	List PR	-	-	No	OCEA
7	Lebanon	BV-Comm	78	9	Yes	ME
8	Netherlands	List PR	10	2	No	WEUR
9	Canada	FPTP	6	2	No	NA
10	Switzerland	List PR	9	2	No	WEUR
11	New Zealand	MMP	20	2	Yes	OCEA
12	Slovenia	List PR	27	2	Yes	CEEUR
13	Sri Lanka	FPTP	93	6	No	ASIA
14	Finland	List PR	11	2	No	WEUR
15	Kiribati	TRS	-	2	Yes	OCEA
16	Sweden	List PR	5	2	No	WEUR
17	Slovakia	List PR	42	2	No	CEEUR
18	Zambia	FPTP	165	8	No	AFR
19	Malawi	FPTP	166	8	No	AFR
20	Iraq	List PR	-	11	No	ME
21	Albania	MMP	73	6	No	CEEUR
22	Zimbabwe	FPTP	151	13	No	AFR
23	Denmark	List PR	15	2	No	WEUR
24	Papua New Guinea	AV	139	5	No	OCEA
25	Ireland	STV	4	2	No	WEUR
26	Australia	AV	3	2	No	OCEA
27	Norway	List PR	1	2	No	WEUR
28	Mongolia	BV	116	4	No	ASIA
29	Poland	List PR	37	2	No	CEEUR
30	Pakistan	FPTP	134	11	Yes	ASIA
31	Germany	MMP	21	2	No	WEUR
32	Bulgaria	List PR	54	3	No	CEEUR
33	UK	FPTP	18	2	No	WEUR
34	Trinidad & Tobago	FPTP	57	5	No	NA
35	Azerbaijan	PAR	99	11	No	CEEUR
36	Fiji	AV	90	7	Yes	OCEA
37	Romania	List PR	60	4	Yes	CEEUR
38	France	TRS	16	2	No	WEUR
39	India	FPTP	126	5	Yes	ASIA

Rep. rank	Country	Electoral system	HDI ranking	Dem. score	Reserv. seats?	Region
40	**United States**	FPTP	8	2	No	NA
41	**Lithuania**	List PR	41	2	No	CEEUR
42	**Israel**	List PR	23	3	No	ME
43	**Croatia**	List PR	44	4	Yes	CEEUR
44	**Macedonia**	List PR	66	6	No	CEEUR
45	**Afghanistan**	SNTV	-	10	Yes	ASIA
46	**Brazil**	List PR	69	5	No	LA
47	**Spain**	List PR	19	2	No	WEUR
48	**Latvia**	List PR	45	2	No	CEEUR
49	**Estonia**	List PR	40	2	No	CEEUR
50	**Montenegro**	List PR	-	5	No	CEEUR

Sources: Electoral System: See Reynolds, Reilly and Ellis, *Electoral System Design: The New International IDEA Handbook* (Stockholm, International Institute for Democracy and Electoral Assistance, 2005). Reserved Seats: see Andrew Reynolds, 'Reserved seats in national legislatures', *Legislative Studies Quarterly* vol. 25, no. 3 (May 2005). Human Development Index 2006, UNDP: See http://en.wikipedia.org/wiki/List_of_countries_by_Human_Development_Index Democracy Score: See Freedom House 2006: http://www.freedomhouse.org/template.cfm?page=1 5 (scores range from 2, highest democracy score, to 14, lowest).

Status of ratification of major international and regional instruments relevant to minority and indigenous rights

as of October 2006

■ Ratification, accession or succession.

□ Signature not yet followed by ratification.

■▶ Ratification of ICERD and Declaration on Article 14.

■▷ Ratification of ICERD and Signature of Declaration on Article 14.

■● Ratification of ICCPR and Optional Protocol.

■○ Ratification of ICCPR and Signature of Optional Protocol.

□○ Signature of ICCPR and Optional Protocol.

	International Convention on the Prevention and Punishment of the Crime of Genocide 1948	International Convention on the Elimination of All Forms of Racial Discrimination 1965	International Covenant on Civil and Political Rights 1966	International Covenant on Economic, Social and Cultural Rights 1966
Africa				
Algeria	■	■▶	■●	■
Angola			■●	■
Benin		■	■●	■
Botswana		■	■	
Burkina Faso	■	■	■●	■
Burundi	■	■	■	■
Cameroon		■	■●	■
Cape Verde		■	■●	■
Central African Republic		■	■●	■
Chad		■	■●	■
Comoros	■	■		
Congo		■	■●	■
Côte d'Ivoire	■	■	■●	■
Democratic Republic of the Congo			■	■
Djibouti			■●	■
Egypt	■	■	■	■
Equatorial Guinea		■	■●	■
Eritrea		■	■	■
Ethiopia	■	■	■	■
Gabon	■	■	■	■
Gambia	■	■	■●	■
Ghana	■	■	■●	■
Guinea	■	■	■●	■
Guinea Bissau		□	□	■
Kenya		■	■	■
Lesotho	■	■	■●	■
Liberia	■	■	■○	
Libyan Arab Jamahiriya	■	■	■●	■
Madagascar		■	■●	■
Malawi		■	■	■
Mali	■	■	■●	■
Mauritania		■	■	■
Mauritius		■	■●	■
Morocco	■	■	■	■
Mozambique	■	■	■	
Namibia	■	■	■●	■
Niger		■	■●	■

Status of ratification of major international and regional instruments relevant to minority and indigenous rights

as of October 2006

■ Ratification, accession or succession.

□ Signature not yet followed by ratification.

■▶ Ratification of ICERD and Declaration on Article 14.

■▷ Ratification of ICERD and Signature of Declaration on Article 14.

■● Ratification of ICCPR and Optional Protocol.

■○ Ratification of ICCPR and Signature of Optional Protocol.

□○ Signature of ICCPR and Optional Protocol.

	International Convention on the Prevention and Punishment of the Crime of Genocide 1948	International Convention on the Elimination of All Forms of Racial Discrimination 1965	International Covenant on Civil and Political Rights 1966	International Covenant on Economic, Social and Cultural Rights 1966
Nigeria		■	■	■
Rwanda	■	■	■	
Sahrawi Arab Democratic Republic				
São Tomé and Príncipe		□	□○	□
Senegal	■	■▶	■●	■
Seychelles	■	■	■	■
Sierra Leone		■		
Somalia		■	■	■
South Africa	■	■▶	■●	□
Sudan	■	■	■	■
Swaziland		■	■	■
Togo	■	■	■●	■
Tunisia	■	■	■	■
Uganda	■	■	■●	■
United Republic of Tanzania	■	■	■	■
Zambia		■	■●	■
Zimbabwe	■	■	■	■
Americas				
Antigua and Barbuda	■	■		
Argentina	■	■	■●	■
Bahamas	■	■		
Barbados	■	■	■●	
Belize	■	■	■	□
Bolivia	■	■	■●	■
Brazil	■	■▶	■	■
Canada	■	■	■●	■
Chile	■	■▶	■●	■
Colombia	■	■	■●	■
Costa Rica	■	■▶	■●	■
Cuba	■	■		
Dominica			■	
Dominican Republic	□	■	■●	■

Convention on the Elimination of All Forms of Discrimination against Women 1979	Convention on the Rights of the Child 1989	ILO 111 Discrimination (Employment and Occupation) Convention, 1958	ILO 169 Convention Concerning Indigenous and Tribal Peoples in Independent Countries 1989	International Convention on the Protection of the Rights of All Migrant Workers and Members of Their Families 1990	ICC Rome Statute of the International Criminal Court 1998	African Charter on Human and Peoples' Rights 2003	African Charter on the Rights and Welfare of the Child 1990
■	■	■			■	■	■
■	■	■				■	■
							□
■	■	■		□	□	■	
■	■	■		■	■	■	■
■	■	■		■	□	■	■
■	■	■		□	■	■	
	□	■				■	□
■	■	■			■	■	
	■	■			□	■	
■	■	■			■	■	□
■	■	■		□	■	■	■
■	■	■			■	■	□
■	■	■		■	■	■	
■	■	■			■	■	■
■	■	■			■	■	□
■	■	■			□	■	■

Convention on the Elimination of All Forms of Discrimination against Women 1979	Convention on the Rights of the Child 1989	ILO 111 Discrimination (Employment and Occupation) Convention, 1958	ILO 169 Convention Concerning Indigenous and Tribal Peoples in Independent Countries 1989	International Convention on the Protection of the Rights of All Migrant Workers and Members of Their Families 1990	ICC Rome Statute of the International Criminal Court 1998	American Convention on Human Rights 1969	Additional Protocol to the American Convention on Human Rights in the area of Economic, Social and Cultural Rights 1988
■	■	■			■		
■	■	■	■	□	■	■	■
■	■	■			□		
■	■	■			■		
■	■	■		■	■		
■	■	■	■	■	■	■	□
■	■	■	■		■	■	■
■	■	■			■		
■	■	■		■	□	■	□
■	■	■		■	■	■	■
■	■	■	■		■	■	■
■	■	■					
■	■				■	■	
■	■	■	■		■	■	□

Status of ratification of major international and regional instruments relevant to minority and indigenous rights

as of October 2006

■ Ratification, accession or succession.

□ Signature not yet followed by ratification.

■▶ Ratification of ICERD and Declaration on Article 14.

■▷ Ratification of ICERD and Signature of Declaration on Article 14.

■● Ratification of ICCPR and Optional Protocol.

■○ Ratification of ICCPR and Signature of Optional Protocol.

□○ Signature of ICCPR and Optional Protocol.

	Genocide 1948	ICERD 1965	ICCPR 1966	ICESCR 1966
Ecuador	■	■▶	■●	■
El Salvador	■	■	■●	■
Grenada			■	■
Guatemala	■	■	■●	■
Guyana		■	■●	■
Haití	■	■	■	
Honduras	■	■	■●	■
Jamaica	■	■	■●	■
México	■	■▶	■●	■
Nicaragua	■	■	■●	■
Panamá	■	■	■●	■
Paraguay	■	■	■●	■
Perú	■	■▶	■●	■
Saint Kitts and Nevis		■		
Saint Lucia		■		
Saint Vincent and the Grenadines	■	■	■●	■
Suriname		■	■●	■
Trinidad and Tobago	■	■	■●	■
United States of America	■	■	■	□
Uruguay	■	■▶	■●	■
Venezuela	■	■▶	■●	■
Asia				
Afghanistan	■	■	■	■
Bangladesh	■	■	■	■
Bhutan		□		
Brunei Darussalam				
Cambodia	■	■	■○	■
China	■	■	□	■
Democratic People's Republic of Korea	■		■	■
India	■	■	■	■
Indonesia		■	■	■
Japan		■	■	■
Kazakhstan	■	■	■	■
Kyrgyzstan	■	■	■●	■
Lao People's Democratic Republic	■	■	□	□
Malaysia	■			

Convention on the Elimination of All Forms of Discrimination against Women 1979	Convention on the Rights of the Child 1989	ILO 111 Discrimination (Employment and Occupation) Convention, 1958	ILO 169 Convention Concerning Indigenous and Tribal Peoples in Independent Countries 1989	International Convention on the Protection of the Rights of All Migrant Workers and Members of Their Families 1990	ICC Rome Statute of the International Criminal Court 1998	American Convention on Human Rights 1969	Additional Protocol to the American Convention on Human Rights in the area of Economic, Social and Cultural Rights 1988
■	■	■	■	■	■	■	■
■	■	■		■		■	■
■	■	■				■	■
■	■	■	■	■		■	■
■	■	■		□	■		
■	■	■			□	■	□
■	■	■	■	■	■	■	□
■	■	■			□	■	□
■	■	■	■	■	■	■	
■	■	■		■	■	■	□
■	■	■			■	■	■
■	■	■	■	□	■	■	■
■	■	■	■	■	■	■	■
■	■	■			□		
■	■	■			■		
■	■					■	■
■	■	■			■	■	
□	□				□	□	
■	■	■		■	■	■	■
■	■	■	■		■	■	□
■	■	■			■		
■	■	■		□	□		
■	■						
	■						
■	■	■		□	■		
■	■	■					
■	■	■					
■	■	■					
■	■	■		□			
■	■						
■	■						
■	■	■	■	■	□		
■	■						
	■						

Status of ratification of major international and regional instruments relevant to minority and indigenous rights

as of October 2006

■ Ratification, accession or succession.

□ Signature not yet followed by ratification.

■▶ Ratification of ICERD and Declaration on Article 14.

■▷ Ratification of ICERD and Signature of Declaration on Article 14.

■● Ratification of ICCPR and Optional Protocol.

■○ Ratification of ICCPR and Signature of Optional Protocol.

□○ Signature of ICCPR and Optional Protocol.

	International Convention on the Prevention and Punishment of the Crime of Genocide 1948	International Convention on the Elimination of All Forms of Racial Discrimination 1965	International Covenant on Civil and Political Rights 1966	International Covenant on Economic, Social and Cultural Rights 1966
Maldives	■	■		■
Mongolia	■	■	■●	■
Myanmar	■			
Nepal	■	■	■●	■
Pakistan	■	■		□
Philippines	■	■	■●	■
Republic of Korea	■	■▶	■●	■
Singapore	■			
Sri Lanka	■	■	■●	■
Tajikistan		■	■●	■
Thailand		■	■	■
Timor-Leste		■	■	■
Turkmenistan		■	■●	■
Uzbekistan	■	■	■●	■
Viet Nam	■	■	■	■
Europe				
Albania	■	■	■	■
Andorra	■	■	■●	
Armenia	■	■	■●	■
Austria	■	■▶	■●	■
Azerbaijan	■	■▶	■●	■
Belarus	■	■	■●	■
Belgium	■	■▶	■●	■
Bosnia and Herzegovina	■	■	■●	■
Bulgaria	■	■▶	■●	■
Croatia	■	■	■●	■
Cyprus	■	■▶	■●	■
Czech Republic	■	■▶	■●	■
Denmark	■	■▶	■●	■
Estonia	■	■	■●	■
Finland	■	■▶	■●	■
France	■	■▶	■●	■
Georgia	■	■▶	■●	■
Germany	■	■▶	■●	■

Convention on the Elimination of All Forms of Discrimination against Women 1979	Convention on the Rights of the Child 1989	ILO 111 Discrimination (Employment and Occupation) Convention, 1958	ILO 169 Convention Concerning Indigenous and Tribal Peoples in Independent Countries 1989	International Convention on the Protection of the Rights of All Migrant Workers and Members of Their Families 1990	ICC Rome Statute of the International Criminal Court 1998		
■	■						
■	■	■			■		
■	■						
■	■	■					
■	■	■					
■	■	■		■	□		
■	■	■			■		
■	■						
■	■	■		■			
■	■	■		■	■		
■	■				□		
■	■			■	■		
■	■	■					
■	■				□		
■	■	■					

Convention on the Elimination of All Forms of Discrimination against Women 1979	Convention on the Rights of the Child 1989	ILO 111 Discrimination (Employment and Occupation) Convention, 1958	ILO 169 Convention Concerning Indigenous and Tribal Peoples in Independent Countries 1989	International Convention on the Protection of the Rights of All Migrant Workers and Members of Their Families 1990	ICC Rome Statute of the International Criminal Court 1998	European Charter for Regional or Minority Languages 1992	Framework Convention for the Protection of National Minorities 1995
■	■	■			■		■
■	■				■		
■	■	■			□	■	■
■	■	■			■	■	■
■	■	■		■	□		■
■	■	■					
■	■	■			■		□
■	■	■		■	□		■
■	■	■			■		■
■	■	■			■	■	■
■	■	■			■	■	■
■	■	■			□	■	■
■	■	■	■		■	■	■
■	■	■			■		■
■	■	■			■	■	■
■	■	■			■	□	■
■	■				■		■
■	■	■	■		■	■	■

Status of ratification of major international and regional instruments relevant to minority and indigenous rights

as of October 2006

■ Ratification, accession or succession.

□ Signature not yet followed by ratification.

■▶ Ratification of ICERD and Declaration on Article 14.

■▷ Ratification of ICERD and Signature of Declaration on Article 14.

■● Ratification of ICCPR and Optional Protocol.

■○ Ratification of ICCPR and Signature of Optional Protocol.

□○ Signature of ICCPR and Optional Protocol.

	International Convention on the Prevention and Punishment of the Crime of Genocide 1948	International Convention on the Elimination of All Forms of Racial Discrimination 1965	International Covenant on Civil and Political Rights 1966	International Covenant on Economic, Social and Cultural Rights 1966
Greece	■	■	■●	■
Holy See		■		
Hungary	■	■▶	■●	■
Iceland	■	■▶	■●	■
Ireland	■	■▶	■●	■
Italy	■	■▶	■●	■
Latvia	■	■	■●	■
Liechtenstein	■	■▶		■
Lithuania	■	■	■●	■
Luxembourg	■	■▶	■●	■
Malta		■▶	■●	■
Monaco	■	■▶	■	■
Montenegro	■	■▶	■●	■
Netherlands	■	■▶	■●	■
Norway	■	■▶	■●	■
Poland	■	■▶	■●	■
Portugal	■	■▶	■●	■
Republic of Moldova	■	■	■○	■
Romania	■	■▶	■●	■
Russian Federation	■	■▶	■●	■
San Marino		■	■●	■
Serbia	■	■▶	■●	■
Slovakia	■	■▶	■●	■
Slovenia	■	■▶	■●	■
Spain	■	■▶	■●	■
Sweden	■	■▶	■●	■
Switzerland	■	■▶	■	■
The former Yugoslav Republic of Macedonia	■	■▶	■●	■
Turkey	■	■	■●	■
Ukraine	■	■▶	■●	■
United Kingdom of Great Britain and Northern Ireland	■	■	■	■
Middle East				
Bahrain	■	■	■	
Iran (Islamic Republic of)	■	■	■	■
Iraq	■	■	■	■

Convention on the Elimination of All Forms of Discrimination against Women 1979	Convention on the Rights of the Child 1989	ILO 111 Discrimination (Employment and Occupation) Convention, 1958	ILO 169 Convention Concerning Indigenous and Tribal Peoples in Independent Countries 1989	International Convention on the Protection of the Rights of All Migrant Workers and Members of Their Families 1990	ICC Rome Statute of the International Criminal Court 1998	European Charter for Regional or Minority Languages 1992	Framework Convention for the Protection of National Minorities 1995
							□
■	■	■			■		
	■						■
■	■	■			■	■	□
■	■	■			■	□	■
■	■	■			■		■
■	■	■			■	□	■
■	■	■			■		■
■	■	■			■	■	■
■	■				■		□
■	■	■			■	■	
■	■	■			■	□	
■	■				□		■
■	■	■		■	■	■	■
■	■	■	■		■	■	■
■	■	■	■		■	■	
■	■	■			■	□	■
■	■	■			■		■
■	■	■			□	□	■
■	■	■			■	□	■
■	■	■			□	□	■
■	■	■			■		■
■	■	■		□	■	■	■
■	■	■			■	■	■
■	■	■			■	■	
■	■	■			■	■	
■	■	■			■	■	■
■	■	■			■	□	
■	■	■		■			■
■	■	■			□	■	■
■	■	■			■	■	
■	■	■			□		
■	■	■			□		
■	■	■					

Sources:
http://www.unhchr.ch/tbs/doc.nsf/Statusfrset?OpenFrameSet
http://www.iccnow.org/countryinfo/worldsigsandratifications.html
Treaty Office on http://conventions.coe.int/
http://www.achpr.org/
http://www.cidh.oas.org/
http://www.oas.org/juridico/english/Sigs/b32.html

Status of ratification of major international and regional instruments relevant to minority and indigenous rights

as of October 2006

■ Ratification, accession or succession.

□ Signature not yet followed by ratification.

■▶ Ratification of ICERD and Declaration on Article 14.

■▷ Ratification of ICERD and Signature of Declaration on Article 14.

■● Ratification of ICCPR and Optional Protocol.

■○ Ratification of ICCPR and Signature of Optional Protocol.

□○ Signature of ICCPR and Optional Protocol.

	International Convention on the Prevention and Punishment of the Crime of Genocide 1948	International Convention on the Elimination of All Forms of Racial Discrimination 1965	International Covenant on Civil and Political Rights 1966	International Covenant on Economic, Social and Cultural Rights 1966
Israel	■	■	■	■
Jordan	■	■	■	■
Kuwait	■	■	■	■
Lebanon	■	■	■	■
Oman		■		
Qatar		■		
Saudi Arabia	■	■		
Syrian Arab Republic	■	■	■	■
United Arab Emirates	■	■		
Yemen	■	■	■	■
Oceania				
Australia	■	■▶	■●	■
Cook Islands				
Fiji	■	■		
Kiribati				
Marshall Islands				
Micronesia (Federated States of)				
Nauru		□	□	
New Zealand	■	■	■●	■
Niue				
Palau				
Papua New Guinea	■	■		
Samoa				
Solomon Islands			■	■
Tonga	■	■		
Tuvalu				
Vanuatu				

Convention on the Elimination of All Forms of Discrimination against Women 1979	Convention on the Rights of the Child 1989	ILO 111 Discrimination (Employment and Occupation) Convention, 1958	ILO 169 Convention Concerning Indigenous and Tribal Peoples in Independent Countries 1989	International Convention on the Protection of the Rights of All Migrant Workers and Members of Their Families 1990	ICC Rome Statute of the International Criminal Court 1998		
■	■	■			□		
■	■	■			■		
■	■	■			□		
■	■	■					
□	■				□		
	■	■					
■	■	■					
■	■	■		■	□		
■	■	■			□		
■	■	■			□		
■	■	■			■		
■	■						
■	■	■	■		■		
■	■						
■	■				■		
■	■						
	■				■		
■	■	■			■		
	■						
■	■	■					
■	■				■		
■	■				□		
	■						
■	■						
■	■	■					

Appendices

Declaration on the Rights of Persons Belonging to National or Ethnic, Religious and Linguistic Minorities

Adopted by General Assembly resolution 47/135 of 18 December 1992

The General Assembly,

Reaffirming that one of the basic aims of the United Nations, as proclaimed in the Charter, is to promote and encourage respect for human rights and for fundamental freedoms for all, without distinction as to race, sex, language or religion,

Reaffirming faith in fundamental human rights, in the dignity and worth of the human person, in the equal rights of men and women and of nations large and small,

Desiring to promote the realization of the principles contained in the Charter, the Universal Declaration of Human Rights, the Convention on the Prevention and Punishment of the Crime of Genocide, the International Convention on the Elimination of All Forms of Racial Discrimination, the International Covenant on Civil and Political Rights, the International Covenant on Economic, Social and Cultural Rights, the Declaration on the Elimination of All Forms of Intolerance and of Discrimination Based on Religion or Belief, and the Convention on the Rights of the Child, as well as other relevant international instruments that have been adopted at the universal or regional level and those concluded between individual States Members of the United Nations,

Inspired by the provisions of article 27 of the International Covenant on Civil and Political Rights concerning the rights of persons belonging to ethnic, religious and linguistic minorities,

Considering that the promotion and protection of the rights of persons belonging to national or ethnic, religious and linguistic minorities contribute to the political and social stability of States in which they live,

Emphasizing that the constant promotion and realization of the rights of persons belonging to national or ethnic, religious and linguistic minorities, as an integral part of the development of society as a whole and within a democratic framework based on the rule of law, would contribute to the strengthening of friendship and cooperation among peoples and States,

Considering that the United Nations has an important role to play regarding the protection of minorities,

Bearing in mind the work done so far within the United Nations system, in particular by the Commission on Human Rights, the Subcommission on Prevention of Discrimination and Protection of Minorities and the bodies established pursuant to the International Covenants on Human Rights and other relevant international human rights instruments in promoting and protecting the rights of persons belonging to national or ethnic, religious and linguistic minorities,

Taking into account the important work which is done by intergovernmental and non-governmental organizations in protecting minorities and in promoting and protecting the rights of persons belonging to national or ethnic, religious and linguistic minorities,

Recognizing the need to ensure even more effective implementation of international human rights instruments with regard to the rights of persons belonging to national or ethnic, religious and linguistic minorities,

Proclaims this Declaration on the Rights of Persons Belonging to National or Ethnic, Religious and Linguistic Minorities:

Article 1

1. States shall protect the existence and the national or ethnic, cultural, religious and linguistic identity of minorities within their respective territories and shall encourage conditions for the promotion of that identity.
2. States shall adopt appropriate legislative and other measures to achieve those ends.

Article 2

1. Persons belonging to national or ethnic, religious and linguistic minorities (hereinafter referred to as persons belonging to minorities) have the right to enjoy their own culture, to profess and practise their own religion, and to use their own language, in private and in public, freely and without interference or any form of discrimination.
2. Persons belonging to minorities have the right to participate effectively in cultural, religious, social, economic and public life.
3. Persons belonging to minorities have the right to participate effectively in decisions on the national and, where appropriate, regional level concerning the minority to which they belong or the regions in which they live, in a manner not incompatible with national legislation.

4. Persons belonging to minorities have the right to establish and maintain their own associations.

5. Persons belonging to minorities have the right to establish and maintain, without any discrimination, free and peaceful contacts with other members of their group and with persons belonging to other minorities, as well as contacts across frontiers with citizens of other States to whom they are related by national or ethnic, religious or linguistic ties.

Article 3

1. Persons belonging to minorities may exercise their rights, including those set forth in the present Declaration, individually as well as in community with other members of their group, without any discrimination.

2. No disadvantage shall result for any person belonging to a minority as the consequence of the exercise or non-exercise of the rights set forth in the present Declaration.

Article 4

1. States shall take measures where required to ensure that persons belonging to minorities may exercise fully and effectively all their human rights and fundamental freedoms without any discrimination and in full equality before the law.

2. States shall take measures to create favourable conditions to enable persons belonging to minorities to express their characteristics and to develop their culture, language, religion, traditions and customs, except where specific practices are in violation of national law and contrary to international standards.

3. States should take appropriate measures so that, wherever possible, persons belonging to minorities may have adequate opportunities to learn their mother tongue or to have instruction in their mother tongue.

4. States should, where appropriate, take measures in the field of education, in order to encourage knowledge of the history, traditions, language and culture of the minorities existing within their territory. Persons belonging to minorities should have adequate opportunities to gain knowledge of the society as a whole.

5. States should consider appropriate measures so that persons belonging to minorities may participate fully in the economic progress and development in their country.

Article 5

1. National policies and programmes shall be planned and implemented with due regard for the legitimate interests of persons belonging to minorities.

2. Programmes of cooperation and assistance among States should be planned and implemented with due regard for the legitimate interests of persons belonging to minorities.

Article 6

States should cooperate on questions relating to persons belonging to minorities, inter alia, exchanging information and experiences, in order to promote mutual understanding and confidence.

Article 7

States should cooperate in order to promote respect for the rights set forth in the present Declaration.

Article 8

1. Nothing in the present Declaration shall prevent the fulfilment of international obligations of States in relation to persons belonging to minorities. In particular, States shall fulfil in good faith the obligations and commitments they have assumed under international treaties and agreements to which they are parties.

2. The exercise of the rights set forth in the present Declaration shall not prejudice the enjoyment by all persons of universally recognized human rights and fundamental freedoms.

3. Measures taken by States to ensure the effective enjoyment of the rights set forth in the present Declaration shall not prima facie be considered contrary to the principle of equality contained in the Universal Declaration of Human Rights.

4. Nothing in the present Declaration may be construed as permitting any activity contrary to the purposes and principles of the United Nations, including sovereign equality, territorial integrity and political independence of States.

Article 9

The specialized agencies and other organizations of the United Nations system shall contribute to the full realization of the rights and principles set forth in the present Declaration, within their respective fields of competence.

Appendices

Who are Minorities?

There is no universally accepted definition of 'minorities', and the word is interpreted differently in different societies. The United Nations (UN) has failed to agree a definition of what constitutes a minority, beyond that implied in the title of the UN Declaration on the Rights of Persons belonging to National or Ethnic, Religious and Linguistic Minorities. Attempting a more precise statement has been fraught with difficulties: in some cases the motivation for a tighter definition has been to deny certain rights to certain peoples.

Minority Rights Group International (MRG) focuses its work on non-dominant ethnic, religious and linguistic communities, who may not necessarily be numerical minorities. MRG's work includes initiatives with indigenous and tribal peoples, migrant communities and refugees. These communities may not wish to be classified as minorities for various reasons. We also recognize that these groups are not homogeneous – some members face further marginalization due to age, class, disability, gender or other factors.

The groups MRG works with are among the poorest and most marginalized groups in society. They may lack access to political power, face discrimination and human rights abuses, and have 'development' policies imposed upon them. MRG seeks to protect and promote the basic rights of these communities. We believe that recognition of minority and indigenous peoples' rights is crucial to establishing and maintaining just and peaceful societies.

Contributors

Maurice Bryn is a Caribbean-born writer and communications consultant. Over the past two decades he has worked in a variety of countries in Latin America, the Caribbean, Asia and Africa. This included examining the role of history, culture and information technology in facilitating a rights-based approach to social and economic change. He currently spends most of his time in Central America.

Dr Joshua Castellino is Professor of Law at the Transitional Justice Institute, University of Ulster, Northern Ireland. He completed his PhD in International Law at the University of Hull, in 1998. A former journalist in India, he specializes in minority rights, international and human rights law, and has authored three books on these subjects. He has extensive experience of involvement on issues concerning minority rights at intergovernmental and NGO levels.

Emma Eastwood has spent over a decade working in the field of human rights protection in Latin America as an international observer and Communications Officer with Peace Brigades International. She is currently working as media and events officer at Minority Rights Group International.

Dr Kristin Henrard is associate professor at the University of Groningen and academic coordinator of the Human Rights specialization within the existing LLM in International and European Law. Since February 2005 she has been working on a project regarding the implications for minority protection of the Race Directive. She is a member of the Young Academy of the Royal Dutch Academy of Sciences, managing editor of the *Netherlands International Law Review*, and is on the international advisory board of the *Global Review of Ethnopolitics*.

Mark Lattimer is the Executive Director of Minority Rights Group International. Formerly with Amnesty International, his recent publications include (as Editor) *Genocide and Human Rights* (Ashgate, 2007) and (with Philippe Sands QC), *Justice for Crimes Against Humanity* (Oxford, Hart, 2003).

Gay J. McDougall is the United Nations Independent Expert on minority issues. A human rights lawyer, she was formerly Executive Director of Global Rights and served on the UN Committee on the Elimination of Racial Discrimination (CERD). She was one of five international members of South Africa's Independent Electoral Commission, which successfully organized and administered that country's first non-racial elections.

Farah Mihlar has worked as a journalist for international organizations including Reuters, Times of India and BBC World Service. She covered Sri Lanka for more than ten years, reporting extensively on the conflict. In the past few years she has worked as a consultant media officer in human rights organizations including the Office of the High Commissioner for Human Rights (OHCHR) and the International Commission of Jurists (ICJ). She currently works as press officer at Minority Rights Group International.

Marusca Perazzi is Programmes Officer and Executive Assistant to the Director at Minority Rights Group International. She holds an MA in Global Governance from the University of Reading and an MA in Diplomacy and International Relations from the University of Padua.

Dr Hugh Poulton is an independent scholar and writer, and a specialist in human and minority rights in South-East Europe. His books include: *The Balkans: Minorities and States in Conflict* (1991, 1993); *Who Are the Macedonians?* (1995, 2000); *Top Hat, Grey Wolf and Crescent: Turkish Nationalism and the Turkish Republic* (1997); and an edited volume *Muslim Identity and the Balkan State* (1997).

Andrew Reynolds is Associate Professor of Political Science at the University of Chapel Hill, North Carolina. His research and teaching focus on democratization, constitutional design and electoral politics. He has worked for the United Nations, the International Institute for Democracy and Electoral Assistance, the US State Department and many other organizations. He has served as a consultant on issues of constitutional design for 16 countries.

Eric A. Witte is a senior associate at the Democratisation Policy Council, a trans-Atlantic initiative for accountability in democracy promotion. He served as political adviser to the chief prosecutor at the Special Court for Sierra Leone, and previously worked at policy NGOs in Washington, DC, including the Coalition for International Justice and International Crisis Group. He holds an MA in political science from the Universität Regensburg, Germany.

A report of this size also involves contributions from a large number of other individuals including MRG staff, whose expertise and advice was invaluable. Special thanks to the anonymous reviewers of the different sections, and to Richie Andrew for production coordination and Sophie Richmond for copy editing.

Select Bibliography

Fund for Peace/Foreign Policy, *Failed States Index*, Fund for Peace and Carnegie Endowment for International Peace, 2006, http://www.fundforpeace.org/programs/fsi/fsindex.php

Harff, B., 'No lessons learned from the Holocaust? Assessing risks of genocide and political mass murder since 1955', *American Political Science Review* 97(1), 2003.

Heidelberg Institute for International Conflict Research, *Conflict Barometer 2006*, University of Heidelberg, 2006.

Kaufmann, D., Kraay, A. and Mastruzzi, M., World Bank Institute, *Governance Indicators for 1996–2005*, World Bank, Washington DC, 2006

Marshall, M.G., *Major Episodes of Political Violence 1946–2006*, Center for Systemic Peace, 2006.

Marshall, M.G., and Gurr, T.R., *Peace and Conflict 2005: A Global Survey of Armed Conflicts, Self-Determination Movements, and Democracy*, Center for International Development and Conflict Management (CIDCM), University of Maryland, 2005.

Organisation for Economic Co-operation and Development, *Country Risk Classifications of the Participants to the Arrangement on Officially Supported Export Credits*, www.oecd.org, 2006.